Sunshine and Ice
Volume 11

AMAZING MESSAGES

MARTIN MONEY

New Generation Publishing

AMAZING MESSAGES

Part One

May to September 2015

INTRODUCTION – SPIRITUAL CONCEPTS

It's difficult to imagine Adolf Hitler as an angel. Or Myra Hindley or Jack the Ripper. But in the deepest recesses of their souls they were.

So are you, and me, and everyone else who lives, has ever lived or will at some time live on this planet.

Really? Are you sure? Well, the way I understand it, that's the bottom line for Michael G Reccia, author of the Joseph Communications books.

Granted, he doesn't mention any of history's bad apples by name – that was my idea to vividly make a point. And what a mind-blowing and profound point it is.

For those who haven't read my last book, *Glittering Stars*, Reccia is a medium who claims to channel Joseph, an ancient and highly-evolved spiritual entity who's made contact to impart divine wisdom and warn people we're heading for apocalypse if we don't change our ways fast.

I know what some may be thinking and yes, I agree this does sound doom-laden and highly suspect, the sort of stuff to be taken with a bucket of salt.

But it's not at all alarmist and is in fact full of hope and joy. Honest – check out these books and you'll see what I mean.

No matter where it comes from, there's a comforting and authoritative air to what this guy's saying. There's a subtlety, refinement and great intelligence sadly missing from many religious texts and the ways they're often interpreted.

Joseph, via Michael, asserts that each of our flesh and blood bodies contains a spirit, a soul, that's a tiny part of God, the great Oneness, the primary and eternal energy coursing through our universe and others beyond the stars.

These tiny expressions of the ultimate consciousness are actually in essence beings of light and sound, colour and love – angels, for want of a better word.

The Earth that we see as a big dirty rock hurtling through space is itself a dazzling ball of light and energy but this fact is largely hidden from us by conventional reality.

We, and it, are far older in our accepted framework of time than scientists have estimated and what started out as a divine experiment countless aeons ago ended up going horribly wrong.

The original idea, according to Joseph, was for these small parts of the Whole to explore, examine and report back to God – again, just a convenient label – how they reacted and interacted in this sphere of reality – at that time far more airy, beautiful and infused with light and colour than it appears now.

But in handling this wonderful matrix of experience, the angelic beings slipped up and created a Frankenstein monster of a reality that became hard-edged, messy, badly flawed and beset by all the ugliness, harsh divisions, strife and violence we now see.

And it's in this reality that we struggle to live and have real problems coping with. We end up confused and frustrated, screwing up badly, hurting each other, bickering and falling out on every scale from the personal to the global.

Our own spiritual essences, or souls, wrapped in apparently solid human form, are fighting a constant inner battle against the very strong and persistent negative current that infests our fractured, flawed environment and intrudes deep into our very beings.

It's also the reality that produces individuals so corrupted by this dark, highly destructive energy that they turn seemingly downright evil – like Hitler, Hindley or the Ripper. (That's my interpretation, anyway.)

Even though essentially we're all angels – yes, even them. But we've forgotten.

The Earth as we know it has already suffered two cataclysms and each time, harsh physicality has been swept away and the eternal spiritual beings left temporarily homeless have had to start again from scratch, says Joseph.

But I'm trying to convey deep spiritual concepts in relatively crude, chunky, clumsy words. I love words – they can be beautiful. But their beauty is a pale reflection of the greater and far more striking beauty of the ultimate realities being addressed here.

I'm probably making a right hash of trying to get across in my own pathetically inadequate way the amazing message of these fascinating joyous and enlightening books. Get hold of them for yourself and you'll hopefully see what I'm getting at.

The three I've got are called *Revelation*, *The Fall* and *Your Life After Death*, all published by Band of Light Media.

But a word of warning – they're deep, really deep. I can only grasp the rough gist of what they're saying, and I'm probably getting much of it skew-whiff in passing it on.

All I know is my heart is telling me there's great wisdom and compassion at work here. The assertions are erudite and comprehensive. From a divine source? I'd say so.

Atheists don't believe in God as portrayed in conventional religions. But even they can't argue against the existence of consciousness and energy. And I'd maintain that these are two expressions of the all-embracing primary source of all.

With those thoughts in mind, I feel it's time to continue my haphazard life journal and start *Sunshine and Ice Volume Eleven*. The title will come when I've thought of one.

So here goes…

CHAPTER ONE
METAPHYSICAL MEANDERING

May 18 – Well, I've just posted off a memory stick to Author Essentials holding the completed *Sunshine and Ice Volume Ten – Glittering Stars*, so they can work on that book and publish it in due course.

Welcome to volume eleven…

I was in the Bell yesterday evening and members of the local women's rugby team were having a raucous night out. A thought resurfaced in my mind that I've pondered quite a few times before. And it was this:

One woman on a mission is a daunting prospect – two on the same mission is a terrifying sight. Ha ha! – Only joking girls. Where would we blokes be without you?

It was a fun session as it goes as I chatted to my mate John Gaynor and others. Bev Jones, Tim Robbins and Penny Williams were there and, of course, guv'nors Mark Evans, Laura Williams and deejay Ross Maslin.

Plus several motorcycle riders – Sunday being bikers' night as well as the weekly karaoke. On the face of it an odd combination, but it seems to work.

May 22 – An earthquake has hit Kent. Yes, Kent, England! Gordon Bennett, Mother Earth really is flexing her muscles, isn't she?

Buildings in an area taking in Margate, Canterbury and Southend-on-Sea in next-door Essex shook as residents were woken last night by the 4.2 magnitude tremor, which they thought was a bomb or a plane crash.

No injuries or structural damage were reported, say local police. But it's still shocking that an event usually associated with other countries has occurred so close to home – quite literally for some.

Does this indicate an increasing instability in the Earth's crust, a dark portent of things to come? Who knows?

Okay, I realize it's not unknown for tremors to affect areas in the UK every now and then. But it's hardly normal, or at least hasn't been since pre-historic times. Until now, it seems.

Climate change, a sign of a looming apocalypse, both or neither? Answers on a postcard please.

Purely coincidentally, I read something in one of Michael G Reccia's books the other day that said earthquakes, tremors and shifting tectonic plates were evidence that our planet was exercising its true inner nature as an ever-changing light and airy "aura of possibility" rather than the heavy, dense and rigid mass of matter we see.

He claims humans are similarly a lot less solid and inflexible by original nature – we too are beings of light but we've also become enmeshed in a powerful illusion of reality typified by flesh and bones, stone, metal, plastic and so on.

I had one of those light-bulb moments while reading part of his book *The Fall* yesterday evening.

I've referred frequently in my own writings to positive and negative vibes, currents and energies – interchangeable words for the same thing.

Generally speaking, I see positive as good and negative as bad. I aim to promote and enhance the positive forces of love, light, joy and harmony and help disperse the negative ones of hatred, darkness, misery and division.

But I accept it's not quite that simple and we need both aspects of such polarities to appreciate each one's advantages – just like light and darkness, male and female and yin and yang.

Like I said, I take both viewpoints but I've had trouble reconciling them sometimes – until now. Reccia, apparently guided by Joseph, explains it so eloquently it's like finding that crucial missing piece of a jigsaw puzzle.

A real a-ha moment if ever I had one.

He explains that when the original beings of light – the angels that are in truth us – intensified their Earth plane experiment in manipulating denser matter with a view to reporting their experiences back to the Godhead and helping enhance and evolve the Whole, they accidentally created a serious imbalance.

They did this by using up so much of the positive energy needed for creation that it left behind a disproportionate amount of redundant negative energy that began to corrode the whole matrix in a very destructive way.

Think of electricity. We need both positive and negative currents. Or, consider the Chinese yin and yang symbol – a representation of perfect balance.

The white part has a small black dot in the centre, the black part a tiny white dot – each contains the essence of the other with the two halves constantly growing and diminishing, maintaining a vital equilibrium.

Another example of this is the cycle of the seasons. In the depths of winter darkness and decay lies the seed of new life that'll grow and burst forth again in the spring sun and reach its zenith in summer, to wither and diminish again in autumn and seemingly disappear in winter, to then start all over again.

To get back to Reccia, he says that God's energy – the driving force behind the entire cosmos – is a blend of positive and negative energy. Each needs the other – like men and women, artists and scientists, risk-takers and pragmatists, and so on.

It was that totally innocent but terrible mistake way back through the mists of time that left the Earth in its screwed-up state with too much negative energy and not enough positive.

You know, reading these Joseph Communications books has proper re-ignited my own sense of the spiritual.

My feet are still stuck firmly in the thick, dirty muck of badly flawed physical reality but my head is once again soaring to the heights of cloudless skies, joy and freedom thanks to the wise and illuminating words I'm encountering. It feels so flipping good!

It seems for years I've been pre-occupied with the mundane and far too influenced by the destructively negative.

Don't get me wrong – I've enjoyed some glorious and exquisite moments with family and friends, but I maintain that times like that transcend so-called normal reality to briefly reach a beautiful higher one.

Loving couples, wonderful acts of compassion and seeing people having fun are other aspects of this terrific higher reality which is humanity's natural place in the great scheme of things. Artistry and vistas, words and music, tasty food and nice smells too.

Stuff pain and misery, illness and friction – pause and enjoy those roses, then party! After all, that's what we're here for.

And when I say party, I don't mean getting off our heads – though that can be nice too. No, I'm talking about enjoying life. Each day's a blessing and each second counts, even if you're leading a relatively quiet and uneventful existence like mine.

Granted, an earthquake in Kent isn't as devastating as one in Nepal, and there are millions of people suffering in all sorts of nightmare situations across the globe. Savagery and destruction are rife. In that respect, I count myself very, very lucky.

But every single one of those situations is the product of the experiment that went so badly wrong many moons ago – well, before moons existed actually.

The good news is that even if everything looks really bleak and our physical bodies are racked by pain, our spirits are eternal and destined for far greater things in the afterlife. Better things than we could possibly imagine.

Phew! – After all that metaphysical meandering, it's time to return to the mundane and have a bite to eat.

But before I do that, I'll just proudly announce that it's coming up to the second anniversary of the release of *Sunshine and Ice Volume One – Chronicles of a Lost Soul*, in both paperback form and on Kindle. I received my copies through the post two years ago today. Very cool!

May 24 – It's our second Bank Holiday in May and I had a fun chat, drinks and laughs session round Sam and Carl's on Friday with them, Bec, Rudy, Bailey, Jimmy, a guy called Matty who Bec's now seeing and Albert, her little dog.

Sweden won the Eurovision Song Contest last night for the sixth time while the UK did dismally yet again.

The Middle East continues to be torn apart by war and it's the 29th anniversary of the day I got married. That's life I guess.

May 26 – Yesterday finished off the bank holiday weekend nicely – Sam and Carl had another barbecue. It was overcast but warm and dry.

Apart from them, their boys Rudy and Bailey, Sam's daughter Bec and Albert the dog, others attending included Kelly Adams and her children, her man Matt, Bec's dad Russell Hall, Jem Hannen, Bec's feller Matty, Jimmy, his daughter Molly and his auntie. Very pleasant it was too – cheers guys!

May 31 – I was back at Sam's for another drinkies, music and laughter session yesterday, this time involving her cousin Diane.

Albert the dog and the family's pet cats and rabbits also featured at certain points.

June 1 – Last night I went to the Bell and had a couple of pints with John Gaynor, John Palmer, Matt Brant, Dani Knight, Laura

Williams, Mark Evans and others. Nostalgia reigned as DJ Ross Maslin played some cool old school dance classics.

June 2 – Gordon bleedin' Bennett – yet another boat tragedy! Five people are known to have died and hundreds are missing after a cruise ship carrying more than 450 people capsized on the Yangtze River in China yesterday.

But today's telly news is dominated by the death of former Liberal Democrat Party leader Charles Kennedy at his Fort William home in Scotland. He was just 55.

Tributes have poured in from across the political spectrum for a popular and well-respected man who served as a Member of Parliament for 32 years.

He lost his seat in the SNP landslide in last month's general election.

Mr Kennedy was the youngest sitting MP when first elected in 1983 and led his party from 1999 to 2006, when he resigned after revealing he had been receiving treatment for a long-standing alcohol problem.

Known for his sense of humour and humanity, "Chat Show Charlie" was a proud Scot and fervent opponent of the Iraq War. He was widely liked and I must say he seemed a thoroughly decent bloke to me. He will be greatly missed.

In other news, a 13-year-old girl has gone missing in Mansfield, Nottinghamshire. We all hope and pray for her safe return.

Last night I watched the *Theory of Everything*, the film about pioneering cosmologist Professor Stephen Hawking that won Eddie Redmayne a best actor Oscar for his outstanding performance as the living legend.

Based on books written by Hawking's wife Jane, it's a marvellous movie telling a heart-warming story of love, hope, resilience and perseverance in the face of a cruel and savagely wasting illness.

Hawking certainly has a brilliant mind but he also has a wonderful sense of humour. He's an atheist who reckons science, logic and mathematics can answer crucial questions about existence far better and more accurately than religion or belief can.

I take a different view but I respect his opinions and think he's a pretty cool guy. It was great when he and physicist Professor Brian Cox took part in Monty Python's reunion show, proving that brainy folk don't need to take themselves too seriously.

My own stance is that religion and science should be complementary, not conflicting. But clever mind-manipulators on both sides of the argument seem insanely desperate to keep us all fighting what is in the end a pointless, time-wasting war.

I have no trouble at all reconciling the two and I'm mystified that others do. Okay, I disagree with Hawking about there being no God – I just think that there's nothing in his calculations or formulas that disproves the presence of some form of God energy.

And I firmly hold that no-one has all the answers, we can all learn from each other and those who smugly believe they and their chums have finally stumbled upon the whole truth of existence and our universe are deluded, potentially dangerous fools.

One of the biggest problems with all this is that science is concerned with cold hard facts about a limited, finite physical reality whereas religion is saturated with vivid, simplistic and frequently misunderstood deep symbolism that tries to convey the far more subtle, complex and infinite ultra-realities beyond.

I find it especially heart-warming when logical, rational scientists confirm what the ridiculed mystics have been telling us for millennia – such as in the quantum physics field where breakthroughs proved that atoms can be in two places at the same time.

A scientific breakthrough dating back quite a bit further was the first successful use of photography. And I've got some photos I love.

One of my favourites is a picture my son Phil took of his son Lucas, then three, sitting on a swing looking up at his dad with a broad smile.

It would be a lovely picture anyway, but what makes it for me – and brings a bit of moisture to my eye – is the fact that Lucas is clutching his little Thomas the Tank Engine model toy in one hand. Beautiful!

Phil thoroughly enjoyed watching Thomas videos with me when he was a boy.

Another photo he took was of his wife Emily and my other two grandchildren, Harvey, four, and baby Chloe, all just about to go down a playground slide together.

Emily's smiling at the camera, Harvey's looking at Chloe and laughing and Chloe herself has her head thrown back and eyes closed, clearly giggling like mad.

A third picture taken by Phil is of Chloe, Lucas and Harvey at someone else's birthday party. They're sat side by side, each cheering with arms aloft. Sweet!

Other family photos I love include the ones taken at Phil and Emily's wedding and several older ones featuring Mum, Dad, Jan, Carol and various other rellies dating back over the years. Plus many snaps of me with a variety of mates. Good times!

June 3 – Oh dear! Police searching for missing 13-year-old Amber Peat have found a body.

Formal identification has yet to take place but they must be pretty sure it's her or they wouldn't have risked causing her family and friends undue distress. Our deepest condolences go out to them.

Also on the news, Sepp Blatter has resigned after 17 years as FIFA president amid allegations of corruption in the ranks of world football's governing body.

June 4 – I learned some very sad news last night. My dear Auntie Joyce, Dad's sister, passed to the next level yesterday. Old and frail, she apparently contracted a fast-acting pneumonia that shut down her physical body incredibly quickly.

So I have to attend yet another family funeral at Bournemouth Crematorium. It takes place on Monday June 15.

My cousin Sandra, daughter of Joyce's deceased brother Bert, told me the tragic tidings. I'll sort out a floral tribute and a charity donation and light a candle on returning home later.

Farewell Auntie – one journey ends but another begins as you're reunited with your husband Fred, my Dad Cyril, your other brothers and the passed-over family.

Joyce's physical demise adds another date to a calendar of mourning for yours truly including the anniversaries of Mum's demise on June 18, her birthday three days later, Dad's passing on June 27 and their wedding anniversary on July 4.

On a happier note, I must extend birthday greetings to Sonia Jamieson, a friend I made through Sam and Carl. Have a great day!

June 5 – Salvagers have now fully righted the boat that capsized on China's Yangtze River four days ago. It's feared more than 400 people died in the tragedy.

The *Eastern Star* cruise ship overturned when caught in a storm. Only 14 of the 456 passengers and crew are known to have survived what looks set to be China's worst shipping disaster in more than 60 years of Communist rule.

The chances of finding anyone still alive are said to be slim. Ye gods!

I watched an interesting documentary on TV last night exposing several so-called faith healers, mediums and psychics as charlatans.

There's no doubt in my mind that there are a lot of unscrupulous people out there cruelly preying on the religious beliefs or trusting gullibility of others to make shed loads of cash. And I say shame on them!

But at the same time I'm convinced there are those who truly can tune into the spirit realms or manipulate natural or supernatural energies.

Magic is real, but sadly there are black magicians bent on mischief or worse, as well as white ones boosting the positive vibrations with altruistic intentions.

Notice I say magic and not illusionism – that's just Paul Daniels' type entertainment.

Callous, selfish con artists certainly walk among us but so do joy-bringing, enlightened healers. Trouble is it's hard to tell them apart sometimes.

It's often said a pretty good indicator is whether the person concerned seeks any kind of payment. I see the point, but even the genuinely gifted need to eat and pay the bills.

One guy featured on last night's programme was an American showman using hidden technology to con devoted Christians into believing he had psychic skills while using the strength of his own mind to convince them he could heal "in Jesus' name."

Dirty rotten scoundrel!

Fake key and spoon benders and those fraudulently claiming to channel ancient spiritual beings were also unmasked in the BBC Four documentary.

And I've often said myself that the most dangerous people in our world are those in positions of great power and influence who are adept at manipulating and twisting our very notions of reality, creating highly effective illusions to their own selfish ends. These folk, deeply infected by the negative energy current, play with all our minds in a massive way – with wide-ranging and devastating consequences.

I'd argue that it actually plays right into such nasty individuals' hands to rashly and foolishly write off all those claiming to have special skills or powers as cheats. Many will be, but some will not.

And, when it comes to Michael G Reccia and Joseph, I fully accept that the idea of a modern-day guy being able to channel a millennia-old entity sounds very implausible. I understand people's scepticism – especially when TV documentaries expose frauds.

But there's such amazing, all-embracing wisdom in Reccia's books it makes me wonder where it does come from. Much of it strikes a chord in me. It feels right.

June 7 – It's Sunday and I've had a nice weekend – a pleasant tonic after last week's sad news about Auntie Joyce.

On Friday I was invited round Sam and Carl's to lap up the warm sunshine in their garden, have a few tinnies and chat with them, Rudy, Bailey, Bec, Diane and Russell.

Albert the loveable mutt, the family's pet cats and rabbits were also there and our mutual friend Rich Jeffrey popped in briefly to donate a set of knives for Alex, a chef in need after his old set was commandeered by someone else.

Last night I went to the Bell to see good local rock covers band Fired Up. A great bonus was seeing so many familiar, friendly faces in the bar at the same time. Cool!

The Women's World Cup football competition kicked off late yesterday with host nation Canada beating China 1-0 and the Netherlands winning against New Zealand by the same score line.

Germany, currently rated the globe's top team, play their first match later today and tournament favourites the USA start their campaign tomorrow.

England's first game is against the much-fancied France on Tuesday. Go girls, do us proud!

16

****

CHAPTER TWO – NATURAL BEAUTY

June 8 – It's 11.15am Monday and I've just returned from a very pleasant stroll in the bright sunshine through Fisherman's Walk to Southbourne cliff top to sit overlooking Bournemouth bay. A slight breeze meant it was nice and warm, not scorching hot.

It's very therapeutic to just enjoy a scene of striking natural beauty like that. You temporarily forget the world's troubles and pain which dominate our daily news.

For example, inhabitants of Singapore and its surrounding area are observing a day of mourning for people killed in an earthquake on Friday.

Sixteen are confirmed dead after the magnitude 6.0 quake, which hit Mount Kinabalu in Sabah state. How awful!

Devastation of a far less serious kind was inflicted by Germany's female footballers as they thrashed the Ivory Coast 10-0 to send out an ominous message to other teams taking part in the Women's World Cup in Canada.

The Japanese are reigning champions but Germany are currently rated the world's number one squad. The good news is that, even though they banged in 10 goals to no reply, they showed weaknesses that better opponents might be able to exploit.

June 8 – later – There's a much-used phrase in common parlance concerning "damaged people". It usually signifies a horrendous aspect of someone's past that's blighted the rest of their life.

But the sad truth is that we're all damaged in various degrees by the words and actions of others. And each of us has imposed physical, mental or emotional hurt on those around us, from the slightly bruising to the seriously destructive.

It's an unavoidable fact of life that we should face, accept and embrace rather than too harshly and hypocritically judge others while choosing to ignore our own failings.

June 9 – The USA girls beat Australia 3-1 in their opening match of the World Cup yesterday. Japan beat Switzerland 1-0 and Nigeria impressively drew 3-3 with the well-rated Swedish side.

I'll be rooting for England later as I watch their game against France, being shown live on BBC Two.

June 10 – France won 1-0 but the Lionesses played well against a side ranked third in the world behind Germany and the USA. Reigning champions Japan take fourth place and Sweden, fifth.

Once regarded as easy prey, our girls have risen to sixth and hopes are high that they'll at least reach the quarter-finals.

The other two teams in our group, Mexico and Columbia, drew 1-1. Wins over both could well put England through to the knockout stage.

Brazil, rated seventh, beat the Korean Republic 2-0 in their first match yesterday. Tournament hosts Canada, who also won their opening match, are placed eighth.

June 11 – Sam and Carl hosted another barbecue in the sun yesterday afternoon. Very nice it was too.

June 14 – I experienced another notable first yesterday, a Saturday, when I attended a baby shower. I didn't even know what a baby shower was until invited to the event a few weeks ago.

My daughter-in-law Emily had to explain to me that it was an occasion to donate gifts and cards to a couple expecting a child.

I must confess this is a new one on me and actually seems a bit strange – to throw a party for a baby that's not even arrived yet.

I'm used to christenings and first birthday parties, which seem to make a lot more sense to me because the infant is actually present.

Having said that, it was a thoroughly enjoyable way to spend an afternoon – a fun-filled shindig in a church hall at Kinson, north Bournemouth.

In attendance were family and friends of the couple, Kayleigh and Aaron Applin.

Kayleigh is Cheryl's daughter – Cheryl being my ex-wife Joe's twin sister. So I guess that makes Kayleigh my niece by marriage.

I think it's quite nice that she still calls me Uncle Martin, even though she's an adult now and Joe and I have been divorced two decades. And it was lovely of her and hubby Aaron to invite me to the baby shower.

Phil, Emily and Chloe were there plus Ben, Cheryl's son, and other members of my wider family. A ball pit, bouncy castle, hot dogs and cake were enjoyed as much by the adults as the youngsters.

I travelled to and from the church hall by taxi and by the time I arrived home early evening I was happily shattered after all the excitement.

So I settled down to have tea and watch England beat Mexico 2-1 in the Women's World Cup. Karen Carney and rising star Fran Kirby, aged 21, scored the goals.

Another win against Columbia on Wednesday could well put our lionesses through to the knockout stage but their group was blown wide open earlier yesterday when Columbia sensationally beat the formidable French side 2-0.

England's footballing men are in action later, playing Slovenia in a qualifier for next year's Euros. With five games played, they're currently top of their table with today's rivals second followed by Switzerland, Lithuania, Estonia and San Marino.

There's a world of difference between restraint and repression. The first is vital, the second potentially lethal.

We all need a certain amount of restraint or we'll run amok with no concepts of decency or responsibility and few boundaries, seriously lacking any form of moral compass. Results – chaos and destruction.

But repression is another thing entirely. Clamping down heavily on perfectly natural, normal human impulses bends people's minds out of shape and twists and perverts their emotions and actions accordingly.

Badly compromised notions of normality are dangerously corrupted as people get confused, frustrated and angry, leading to violence and various types of abuse.

Sexual repression is one of worst kinds as it leads to all manner of unsavoury taboo behaviour as wrongly fettered but persistent impulses force their way to the surface to break out in the most shocking and unacceptable ways imaginable.

And here our old friend dogmatic organised religion is largely to blame with its unhealthy demonization of sex as something dirty and sinful leading to damnation.

Yes, we need guidelines, decency and respect linked to a strong sense of morality but we also need a lot less condemnation and much more common sense and compassion.

Society is at fault here and the sick acts we abhor and punish reflect the sicker aspects of communities where people's ideas and values have been disastrously warped.

June 15 – Roy's boys won 3-2, extending their lead at the top of their group table and further cementing their progress to the Euro finals in a year's time.

Jack Wilshere scored his first two goals in an England shirt and skipper Wayne Rooney notched up his 48th, putting him level with Gary Lineker and one behind all-time record holder Sir Bobby Charlton.

June 16 – In sharp contrast to Saturday's happy baby shower event, I went to a family gathering at the other end of the spectrum yesterday (Monday) – Joyce's funeral.

My sister Carol and hubby David drove over from Selsey, West Sussex and picked me up on the way to Bournemouth Crematorium, the setting for so many fond goodbyes for our dwindling clan.

It was nice to see relatives we very rarely do but oh-so poignant to realize how many of our number were missing having passed over themselves.

We chatted to our cousins John and Eric and were struck how much they reminded us of their fathers, our late Uncles Jack and Bert, Auntie Joyce's brothers.

Our Dad, Cyril, was another brother and there was originally a fourth called Phil, the first-born, who tragically died of a brain haemorrhage aged 21 before we were born.

Cousin Andrew – Jack's son and John's brother – was also there plus Sandra, Bert's daughter and Eric's sister, who did most of the arrangements for the crematorium committal service and the modest wake at the old folks' complex where Joyce, 91, spent her twilight years.

Incidentally, Sandra – Sandy – has always reminded me of Joyce, more in the way she talks and acts than appearance-wise.

She also lives in Southbourne with her feller, Alan, in attendance yesterday along with other relatives and some of Joyce's friends.

In fact when my parents, my late sister Jan and I moved from Slough to Bournemouth in the late 1970s, we started something because Sandy, her parents Bert and Sylvia, Joyce and her late husband Fred all came down to join us, buying and sharing a house just around the corner.

It was lovely yesterday to recall treasured memories of past family get-togethers – photo slide evenings, special occasions and days out involving Joyce, Uncle Fred, and our other aunts, uncles and cousins.

Joyce was the last of her generation to go so it really is the end of an era.

And yes, at times we smiled, laughed even – but Joyce would have wanted it that way because we've always enjoyed each others' company and share the strong Money sense of humour, an excellent defence mechanism against sadness, stress and fear.

I want it to be the same when I go. Like my aunt – and I'd wager the rest of the brood – I wouldn't want people to feel obliged to wear black or be miserable.

If they like black and wish to dress accordingly, fair enough. But it's just another colour and I'd want people to wear what they felt comfortable in.

It's natural to be sad on such occasions and respect and decorum are needed at the funeral service itself, but there's no need to be po-faced and glum – certainly not at the gathering afterwards.

I want people to remember me with a smile, even at the committal, and my wake should be a proper party involving music, laughs, alcohol for those who want it and the enthusiastic exchange of fond memories. A tinge of mourning yes, but that's all.

June 17 – In the intro to this book, I referred to an amazing message. At that point, I was speaking spiritually. But amazing messages can also be beautifully mundane.

Take the Facebook message I got from my son Phil earlier today. It contained a photo he took at the baby shower as he was practising for his group shots outside the venue.

The picture is of me holding Chloe as I stood next to a wall in the bright sunshine. Fortunately, we're both smiling and both looking at the camera. It's lovely and quite wonderfully captures the pure joy of close family ties – an amazing message in itself.

Yeah, family ties – I went to another sun-kissed barbecue at Sam and Carl's yesterday. It was arranged to link in with a brief visit by Sam's son Alex, spending a couple of days in Bournemouth before returning to Wiltshire, where he's a chef.

He loves his job, even though it can be very hard work. I think it's great when people actually enjoy what they do to earn their money and so sad when they don't, spending years resenting their predicament and praying for the next holiday or day off.

So Alex turned up with his dad, Russell, to join Sam, Carl, his little brothers Rudy and Bailey, his sister Becca, her man Mattie and our mutual friend Andy at the shindig. Family ties – priceless!

June 18 – Continuing the theme but on a much more sombre note, it was 18 years ago today that my Mum passed on and it still hurts.

Today is also Sir Paul McCartney's 73rd birthday. Have a fab one Macca, you've earned it!

Last night I watched live TV coverage of England's match against Columbia in the Women's World Cup. They won 2-1 to proceed to the knockout stage as group runners-up. France topped the four-team table after pummelling Mexico 5-0.

Our lionesses' next match is against Norway on Monday, June 22.

June 20 – Flippin' 'eck, what a super surprise! I've just switched on my computer and logged in to Facebook to find a friend request from Paula Carruthers!

Yes, THE Paula, that key woman in my life mentioned several times in my books and at length in the first one, *Chronicles of a Lost Soul/A New Perspective*.

I'm delighted she's got in touch again and doubly delighted to discover that she still lives in Bournemouth. We lost contact years ago and for all I knew she'd moved back home to Carlisle or on to another part of the country.

I eagerly confirmed her friend request and sent her a brief hello message. It would be fantastic to meet up again. I'm guessing she's only just joined Facebook as she seemingly found me through my close pal Theresa Bevis, a mutual FB friend. Sweet!

It's only Saturday morning but already turning into quite a weekend for great results.

But yesterday's was one of those delicious spur of the moment things.

Sam wasn't well so sent me a text moving our usual Friday booze and laughs session to later today. So, at a bit of a loose end, I decided to go to the Bell, sit in the warm sun with a chilled pint or two and check out the new menu they've just started up.

And blow me down! – There, standing in front of me was another blast from the past – my mate Paul Savage, who's their freshly-recruited chef.

I first met Paul yonks ago when he was a barman there. He was part of the old Bell crowd along with Kerry Smith, Claire Kimber, John Gaynor, Jem Hannen, Tina Wilkins, Paul Moran, Dave "Spoon" Perry, Theresa, Paula and others.

In more recent years he's been working in another local pub called The Cranleigh – the other end of Southbourne and a bus ride away from here so I don't frequent it.

It was so cool to see him again yesterday – the first time we'd been face to face for years even though we're in Facebook contact. And the fish and chip meal he served up was superb.

An amiable and funny guy, he's very popular and will fit into the new Bell team just as well as he did the old one.

It was also good to see Jaymi Darragh – another friendly face from those bygone Bell times – plus Kelly Adams, Jade Millen, Sam Rose Lowney, the guv'nors Laura and Mark and a guy I only know as Celtic Nicky, who's been a regular there for years.

June 21 – It's Sunday, the summer solstice and my Mum's birthday. RIP lovely lady.

It's also my friend Flavie's birthday. She and her sister, Linda, have both worked at the Bell and I went to Flavie's wedding when she got hitched to Ian, a guy I know from the pub and silliness sessions round my mate Jem's.

My highly enjoyable weekend continued yesterday afternoon and early evening when I spent a few hours with Sam, Carl and family.

Yesterday evening Germany's footballing heroines beat Sweden 4-1 to reach the quarter-finals of the Women's World Cup.

Today being Father's Day, Phil put a message to me on Facebook this morning from him and the children. Nice!

June 22 – Wishing a very happy birthday to my buddy Steve Yarwood. Have a great one mate!

June 23 – England made history in the Women's World Cup last night by beating Norway 2-1 to reach the quarter-finals.

It's the first time our footballing females, nicknamed the Lionesses, have won a World Cup knockout match.

Now they face host nation Canada's team on Saturday, June 27, with a great chance of getting to the semis.

Norway scored first but our girls came from behind to win it with goals from Steph Houghton and a scorcher from Lucy Bronze.

Elsewhere in the news, Cameron and crew continue to scythe through the welfare state and demonize migrant workers – to warnings of devastating consequences.

Re-iterating his intention to enforce another £12 billion welfare cuts which he asserts are needed to help balance the books, he strongly hinted that this time his main targets would be those receiving tax credits and child benefits.

He said he wanted to stop the "ridiculous merry-go-round" of taking money from the lower paid in taxes then returning it to them in welfare payments.

There's little doubt he meant working people's tax credits and child benefits. As with certain other things he's said over the last five years, on the face of it – the way he presents it at least – it sounds like common sense.

But look who's saying it – a rich Tory boy obsessed with making crude, cruel and cavalier budget cuts regardless of who suffers, safe in the knowledge that he and his chums will continue making tons of cash regardless.

His brutal attitude is also highlighted by the shocking revelation that almost 7,000 health workers from abroad will lose their jobs and be deported over the next five years under new government rules.

The Royal College of Nurses warns that this will leave a massive hole in NHS services – with critical implications for patients.

By Home Office decree, overseas workers can only remain in the UK if they are earning at least £36,000 a year within six years of arriving here. The policy will start to take effect from next year onwards as people not meeting the minimum salary level are thrown out of the country.

Huge numbers of NHS staff are from other countries, mainly Spain, Portugal and the Philippines.

The College points out that the average foreign nurse starts on a salary of £22,000, and even after eight years will still only be earning £28,000.

I share Cameron's concern that there aren't enough home-grown workers in our NHS.

And I think it's crazy that most staff get treated so shabbily for providing invaluable services that for years UK people have swerved, taking other career paths instead, leaving the way wide open for thousands of foreigners to eagerly fill any vacancies.

These angels from abroad have put up with rubbish pay and conditions, long shifts, stroppy patients, demanding doctors and mad bureaucracy – and thank goodness they have, for otherwise the NHS would have collapsed.

It seems incredibly churlish and ungrateful to now come up with this policy at such a late stage – the words stable-door and horse spring to mind.

Well done Cameron's cut-throats – good to see you're still living the Tory dream! Trouble is, for the rest of us it's a nightmare.

June 26 – Top runner Mo Farah's right you know, Quorn mince really does make delicious chilli.

The 32-year-old Somalia-born nationalised Brit is our reigning Olympic, World and European champion in distances including 5000 metres and 10,000 metres.

His chilli con carne statement comes in a TV advert he's been enlisted to make for Quorn, the low-fat, high protein meat substitute used in various products including mince, sausages and burgers.

As previously stated, I eat more of these now in keeping with my healthier diet intended to protect my heart. I also have more white meat such as fish, chicken and turkey, a lot more vegetables and a glass of apple juice most days.

I've cut down drastically on my pie consumption, no longer smoke and try to keep my fat, sugar, salt and alcohol intakes under much stricter control than I used to.

And I find the Quorn items really tasty – as good as the meats they replace. Butchers and passionate carnivores would call this sacrilege, but there it is.

I guess it all boils down to personal taste. We all have our preferences, be they foods, activities or topics of expertise and interest.

Take the Chase, for example, one of my favourite telly programmes at the moment.

Actor and comedian Bradley Walsh is the host of this tea-time quiz show during which each episode has a team of four contestants taking on a Mastermind champion against the clock in an attempt to win cash.

Sometimes I shout at the TV, amazed that the participants don't know the answer to a question I find incredibly easy.

On other occasions I'm equally gobsmacked when they respond correctly without hesitation when I don't even understand the question.

But that's the glory of diversity for you. It would be a dull old world if we were all the same.

June 27, tea-time – It was 31 years ago today that my Dad passed on. Thanks for everything you kind, wise, funny man, I lit a candle for you this morning and also put a little tribute on Facebook.

I've recently got back from a highly enjoyable day out at the beach with my own son, Phil, plus Emily, Chloe and Lucas. My ex-sister-in-law Cheryl and her feller Des joined us for the last part of it.

June 28 – Great news! England last night beat Canada 2-1 to line up a semi-final clash with reigning champions Japan in the Women's World Cup. Jodie Taylor and Lucy Bronze – again – scored the goals.

Victory over the Japanese on Wednesday, July 1 would put them in the final against either Germany or the USA, each with two World Cups to their name already.

Hopes are high that the Lionesses can go all the way and lift the trophy. But whatever happens now, coach Mark Sampson and his squad have done us proud – the most successful female England footie team ever.

The Lionesses' match on Wednesday marks the first time an England side has reached the semis of a global competition in this sport for 25 years – since Gazza, Lineker, Shilton and the rest of Robson's boys were knocked out by eventual tournament winners West Germany on penalties at Italia 90.

Very well done girls – keep it up!

June 29 – Sad tidings! Chris Squire, bass player with rock band Yes, has died at his home in America aged 67 of a rare cancer of the blood and bone marrow.

The Londoner formed Yes in 1968 with singer Jon Anderson. They're in my all-time top 10 of groups. I saw them at the Empire Pool arena, Wembley, in 1977 and they were simply superb.

Another of my favourite bands, The Who, topped the Sunday night bill at this weekend's Glastonbury Festival. There's only Pete Townsend and Roger Daltrey left of the original four, Keith Moon having died in 1978 and John Entwistle in 2002. But with Ringo's son Zak Starkey on drums, they can still cut it live.

As usual, I watched quite a lot of Glasto on TV. Other personal highlights included the brilliant Chemical Brothers, Paul Weller, Clean Bandit, the Libertines, Suede and Paloma Faith, whose rendition of Hendrix's Purple Haze was inspired and wonderful.

I also thoroughly enjoyed Motorhead but couldn't help wondering if Glastonbury is the best festival for heavy metal, far better suited to Reading or Leeds.

Lionel Richie wowed the crowd in the now traditional Sunday tea-time "golden oldie" slot and others appearing included Kanye West, Florence and the Machine, Pharrell Williams, George Ezra, Patti Smith, Rudimental and the Waterboys.

Even the Dalai Lama turned up to boost the spiritual aspect of the event – fantastic!

Meanwhile on the wider world stage murder, mayhem and misery continue to take their toll. More than 30 Brits are now thought to have been among those killed when a gunman opened fire on a Tunisian beach on Friday. It's claimed he belonged to an Islamic State terrorist network.

Cameron's responded with his usual lack of tact or balanced thinking, threatening a violent and crushing retaliation against what he called a "poisonous death cult".

That's right Dave, fan those flames of friction and further demonize Muslims, that'll help defuse the situation – not! Gordon bleeding Bennett!

Talking pointedly of cults and constantly blaming religion and foreigners is a very lazy, simplistic and childish way of tackling complex issues. It's doomed to failure.

Islam has nothing to do with it. Neither has any other faith. People committing these atrocities are murderous political extremists – and so are many of those fighting them.

These cultural and ideological clashes are far too often portrayed as religious wars. And that's a gross insult to the faiths and their millions of peace-loving followers.

There's absolutely no chance of us seeing an end to this fast-spiralling cycle of death and destruction until someone has the sense, guts and decency to effectively address and sort out the underlying problems that cause hostility, division and radicalization.

But it's not going to be Cameron or any of his belligerent sabre-rattling cronies, that's for sure. And that's both depressing and distressing.

Where oh where are the politicians with the vision, integrity and determination to try and find peaceful solutions to the world's troubles? Not in Whitehall, or any other seats of power, it seems.

Meanwhile service personnel and innocent victims will continue to die and suffer horrendous injuries as the mad blood-soaked situation spins out of control. Great!

June 30 – Happy birthday Tom Jones. Have a brilliant one, bro! I text my great mate this morning to wish him all the best. Also happy birthday Gail, Emily's mum.

It's now lunchtime and I've been playing The Who and Paul Weller CDs this morning after being inspired all over again by their excellent Glastonbury sets.

I've inadvertently missed Weller off lists of my favourite lyricists published in earlier volumes. This is a regrettable oversight because he really is very good.

Pete Townsend always features because he's right up there with the all-time greats.

Patti Smith – another rock veteran at Glasto this year – is also a skilled poet, great songwriter and mesmerising performer, as evidenced by the live show I saw her perform at Reading Festival back in 1978. Her set at Worthy Farm on Sunday wasn't bad either.

It's Tuesday and I've been playing some classic Yes tracks over the past couple of days in honour of Chris Squire. RIP bass maestro – thanks for the music!

July 2 – The month started with the hottest day of the year yesterday as the sun blazed down and temperatures soared.

I walked to Boscombe and back during the morning and sat basking in Sam's garden in the afternoon.

It's overcast and very muggy as I write this with sweat rolling down my face and dripping on the computer keyboard.

England's World Cup dreams were shattered last night as fate took a cruel twist.

Out Lionesses were drawing 1-1 with Japan and playing better football when – with just a minute of stoppage time left – Laura Bassett put the ball in her own net while trying to clear a cross from a Japanese player.

It was a horrible way to go out but Laura and her team mates can hold their heads high because they've done very well and thrilled us with some excellent football. Now they face Germany on Saturday, July 4, to decide which team ends up third in the tournament. Japan plays the USA in Sunday's final.

Defence Secretary Michael Fallon is to ask Parliament to back the bombing of Syria as part of our response to the Tunisian shootings.

How sick and warped is that? Using the deaths of Brits on a sun-drenched foreign beach as an excuse to do what he, Cameron and co have been itching to do all along.

Am I the only one who finds it all rather convenient that a gunman said to belong to an Islamic terrorist network opens fire on British tourists abroad and less than a week later we have renewed demands for air strikes in Syria?

We've been bombing Iraq for a while now but a proposal to extend the attack into Syria was previously defeated in the Commons. I said at the time that sooner or later the situation would be manipulated to persuade MPs to back the plan.

The only surprise is that it took so long. As for Fallon, perhaps we should change his title to War Secretary.

But it's not just Syria in the government's sights. They're also targeting people in their own country by cutting their sickness benefits. They're planning to reduce the Employment and Support Allowance by about £30 a week, putting it in line with Jobseekers' Allowance.

I've previously questioned the logic of paying people more when by definition they're not as active as others, therefore not funding quite such busy or costly lifestyles.

So in principle I'm for parity between the welfare payments. But I say JSA should be raised, with extra cash help for anyone struggling to fund medical aids or equipment.

But cut-throat Cameron and his rich pals continue their mad crusade to viciously rob the ill, ageing and disadvantaged – just as they had threatened to.

Who on Earth voted these callous clowns back into power?

It's dreadful to realize that enough uncaring, selfish people must be relatively minted, unaffected or maybe even prospering under the Tories' cruel, crazy and blatantly unfair policies to actually support their unholy, obscene war against other citizens.

July 3 – Happy birthday Suzette, my "adopted" sister.

The nation is to hold a minute's silence today for the victims of the Tunisia shootings.

I've lit a candle and intend to observe the respectful 60 quiet seconds along with millions of others. It takes place at noon, just under an hour away.

Because now isn't the time to debate foreign policy or criticize the dark and dirty politics that spark such horrific, tragic events.

We should suspend all talk of the hard-hearted men and women who stir up friction and hostility while they ruthlessly cash in. Of sleazy leaders, unscrupulous money heads and the bloodlust ideological fanatics they mercilessly exploit.

All that can wait. Now's the time to honour the dead and sympathize with their loved ones, regardless of nationality, skin colour, cultural preferences or religious beliefs.

July 4 – You may have noticed that I'm a great advocate of getting to the root causes of problems in order to successfully resolve them.

I've previously stated that a major part of this is wiping out the unfairness; injustices and inequality that make people feel aggrieved and angry in the first place.

We must also look at the twisted values and severe repression of natural impulses that can lead to great frustration, muddled thinking and bad behaviour.

We have to fully understand the reasons why people commit crimes against others, from violence and robbery to various forms of abuse. We need to look at and eradicate the fraught contexts and messed-up mindsets that spark the trouble.

In addition, I'd suggest making wrongdoers face those they've wronged or their families. This forces them to confront and better comprehend the trauma they've inflicted – a far more effective deterrent than killing them or jailing them indefinitely.

That solves nothing and instead perpetuates an endless spiral of hurt and backlash.

I accept that in a small minority of cases my idea wouldn't work because offenders are too mentally disturbed. Such folk require isolation, maybe deep counselling.

But generally speaking, I stand by what I'm proposing.

Reconciliation sessions also give the injured parties better closure, allowing them to much more successfully move on – especially if they end up with a new appreciation of why their tormentors felt and acted the way they did.

Seeing a situation from someone else's perspective for the first time can be very enlightening and liberating. And the wise will perceive that both criminal and prey are victims of a deeply flawed society and its seriously screwed-up attitudes.

I feel this is the proper way forward to a more tolerant and civilised world where mutual consideration and respect for others and their situations replaces a bolshie head-in-the-sand stance where harsh knee-jerk retaliation only prolongs the misery.

Draw a line and look ahead to a more peaceful, harmonious and trouble-free future, for dwelling on the past only perpetuates the pain.

This applies across the board – from one-on-one incidents to international conflicts.

July 5 – Happy birthday Carl – see you later mate!

England beat Germany 1-0 with an extra-time penalty by Fara Williams. I'll pause a moment to let that sink in. Yes, an English footballing side has defeated a German team in a competitive match for the first time since 2001 – with a penalty kick!

It was heartbreaking when our Lionesses narrowly missed out on the World Cup final thanks to a fluke very late own goal against Japan in the semi-final the other day.

But this more than makes up for it. Let's lay out the facts so we can appreciate the full magnitude of the girls' wonderful achievement.

Although knocked out of this tournament by the USA in the semis, Germany remains the world's top-rated female footballing squad. Eight times European champions, their players have twice won the World Cup. It's the first time an English side has beaten them in 21 encounters.

This victory makes Fara and co the best female football team in Europe and the third in the world behind the USA and Japan, who battle it out in today's final.

It's one of finest performances of all time by an England squad at this sport's senior level – almost as impressive as the men winning their World Cup in 1966.

If all that doesn't lift the country, nothing will. And boy do we need some lifting in these troubled times of ferocious austerity and terrorist atrocities.

Watching Festivals Britannia again yesterday evening before the football made me acutely aware of certain chilling parallels between bygone days and current conflicts.

I've mentioned this BBC television documentary before. I recorded it on my Tivo box when it was repeated last week. It tells the story of our love affair with outdoor summer festivals from the 1950s to now – and how some things have changed and others remain depressingly similar.

There's always been a rebellious, anti-establishment element to these events but it's been largely tamed in recent years.

Once upon a time there were no admission fees and the musicians played for free. Now, people are charged high prices to see glamorous global pop stars as the largely compliant cash-point and smart-phone generation temporarily take to the fields.

How different is that aspect from what it was like back in the day.

The festivals started as jazz gatherings as a bohemian uprising against post-war austerity allied itself to Ban the Bomb marches and other political protest groupings.

The rebel aspect hardened under Thatcher as the peace convoys openly challenged harsh right-wing policies, provoking a government that responded violently – sending in the police to crush any protests by cracking skulls and smashing up mobile homes.

It looked like the dream was over until the rave culture kicked in and the outlawed travellers found new allies in the Ecstasy crowd, re-igniting the festival movement.

A new generation was blatantly defying another oppressive right-wing administration.

But the authorities' iron fist retaliation to domestic unrest and terrorist attacks from the 1970s onwards has pretty much demolished people's civil liberties. Now they're petrified of showing too forceful forms of dissent through fear of savage retribution.

The parallels I see with today's situation stem from the growing concern at harsh austerity measures, reminiscent of the 1950s, and a hatred of brutally unfair Tory policies that penalize and disenfranchise, similar to those inflicted in later decades.

The festivals, largely televised, no longer pose an open threat to the establishment – although many attending them might well be indulging in a mild version of protest.

Consequently, the government doesn't need to crack skulls or trash homes any more. Instead it hits and hurts people in another way – through their pockets, denying them welfare payments they need and should be getting.

The methods of exercising vicious authority have changed. The mindset's the same.

I want to brighten the mood before signing off and having a bite to eat. So I'll end this bit by saying I have various reasons to be very proud of my son Phil. Some are quite light-hearted, others more serious. I don't need to explain this – just say it.

July 6 – But only just, seeing as it's a couple of minutes after midnight.

Two and a bit hours ago I got back from Carl's birthday bash at his and Sam's place. The children Rudy and Bailey were there, plus Alex and Becca, Joedie Watt, Rich Jeffery, Jem Hannen, Sonia Jamieson, Diane, Jimmy and others, plus the family pets. It was a good do, with a barbecue cooked by Alex and the customary booze and fun.

The USA beat Japan 5-2 to take the Women's World Cup. They've won three now – one more than Germany – so they're the number one nation in the contest's history.

Screw it, I've just decided. I love sharing nice, positive stuff but lately I've been so angry at violent events, people's cold and brutal attitudes and our leaders' despicable behaviour I've spent far too much writing time banging on about them.

Enough! From now on I'm gonna concentrate on the lighter side of life. Love, peace harmony and humour, tolerance, acceptance and respect. That sort of thing.

Well, I'll try at least. Don't want to make any rash promises. Watch this space…

****

CHAPTER THREE – A HAPPY REUNION

July 7 – It's Ringo Starr's 75th birthday and the 10th anniversary of the London Bombs. Happy celebration and bitter loss – the two extremes of human existence.

July 7, early evening – I've just had a pretty stupendous time. I met my very good friend Paula Carruthers for a couple of drinks and a catch-up – fantastic!

Readers of my earlier books will appreciate that Paula is a very important person in my life. I'm chuffed to bits we're back in contact after all these years.

We met at lunchtime in a Boscombe pub called the Percy Florence Shelley then went on to the Bell, scene of so many fond memories from our shared past.

It was a very happy reunion and we promised to continue meeting up regularly from now on. Great!

July 8 – Wishing a very happy 25th birthday to Laura, Sam's cousin. I'll be seeing her later at Sam and Carl's when they stage a little party for her.

Drinking two days on the trot – Oh dear! Now I'm gonna have to save myself for Saturday, three days away, when I'll be attending a special charity fun day at the Bell.

I really must apply the brakes to my alcohol consumption as a matter of urgency, for the good of my health but also my finances. Having said that, yesterday was brilliant and today also counts as a special occasion.

July 11, mid-evening – I've just had a quite excellent few hours at the Bell. It was a charity fun day in aid of Homes for Heroes, the organisation that raises money to house ex-service folk who'd otherwise be on the streets.

Some might think it odd, a pacifist like me supporting such a cause. As I've said before, I detest the belligerent impulses that send our brave troops into battle in far-flung foreign parts for decidedly dodgy reasons based on political expediency, commercial greed, imperialistic ambitions or ancient power struggles.

But I wholeheartedly empathize with those in the firing line, caught up in such insanity – those killed or badly damaged and their families. What a waste!

So I happily donate to Homes for Heroes, Help for Heroes and the Royal British Legion. And I see no contradiction between this and my anti-war stance.

Apart from firmly backing the idea behind the day, I had a grand time seeing loads of familiar and friendly faces, including John Palmer, Paul Moran, Jeff McNally, Lou and Chris Davis, Lee Robertson, Jemma Davies, Stu and Melody Moss, Julia Pike, Jem, Martine and Tony Hannen, Billy Clarkson, Mark Hemington and Matt Brant.

Plus guv'nors Laura and Mark, DJs Darren and Ross, some great live music acts and Sam Lowney, a Bell stalwart who worked so hard to make the event a success.

The weather was nice, a great help since most of the fund-raising activities took place in the beer garden. I was really pleased for Mark and Laura, and especially for Sam, who thoroughly deserved the day to be the undoubted triumph that it was.

Well done Nicola, Callum and the other bar staff too who kept the booze flowing.

I love my local pub!

July 15 – Once again there are some interesting items on the daily news.

Legislation tightening the rules on strike action is to be announced in the Commons later today. The Trade Union Bill proposes minimum turnouts in strike ballots, time limits on mandates for industrial action and changes to political levies.

The government says this will balance the right to strike with the rights of working people and businesses.

I'm all for keeping a balance and my opposition to the old closed shops is well documented. People's ability to guard against exploitation should be weighed against their freedom of choice not to join a union or withdraw labour if that's their wish.

Unions offer invaluable protection and strength in numbers when negotiating pay rises and working conditions. And a lot of bosses prefer to deal with one single united body rather than numerous individuals all trying to secure their own deals.

But if someone wants to go it alone and agree their own terms of employment with their company they should be allowed to.

They wouldn't benefit from any union-boss agreements and they could be wide open to the whims of the unscrupulous. If they want to take that risk, let them I say.

And there's no doubt the big closed-shop unions used to be far too powerful, able to hold the country to ransom and make life a misery for other hard-pressed fellow workers at the drop of a hat.

These uncaring and greedy organisations selfishly grabbed the lion's share of the nation's industrial cake, leaving other smaller unions to scrap and scrabble for the few crumbs left – and I found that morally reprehensible.

They needed reigning in for sure – but then Thatcher came along with her sledgehammer and obliterated them, leaving them far too weak and ineffective.

She smashed civil rights generally and union power in particular.

Cameron and his right-wing government are just carrying on where she left off. It's despicable – we've already gone way too far towards the other extreme of no citizens' or workers' rights whatsoever.

And, to state the bleeding obvious, if employers treated staff decently and fairly there would be no need for unions anyway.

This is the proper way forward surely? – turning the legislation on its head to actually outlaw the ruthless exploitation of people using low pay and poor conditions.

For a happy worker is a productive worker willing to use their time and energy for the common good of helping make the firm a success for everyone's benefit.

All this seems so obvious to me. Sadly, not so for many bosses and certainly not the MPs coming up with these punitive laws guaranteed to cause resentment and rage.

While we're on the subject of firms and work, another item on today's news told us that the UK jobless total had risen for the first time in two years.

Ha ha! Gotcha Cameron!

The Office for National Statistics (ONS) said unemployment in the March to May period totalled 1.85 million, up 15,000 from the previous quarter.

Don't you find it strange how we're only hearing about this after an election in which Cameron and crew conned people into voting for them with their wild claims that the economy was improving and unemployment falling, thanks to them.

I don't trust any figures put out by this lot anyway. I just see the devastation their brutal policies have had on our nation and in particular the people around me.

Have you noticed that the word conservative starts with the smaller word con, meaning to dupe or trick. Says it all really, don't you think?

Keeping with the news, there's been a lot said over the past few weeks about Greece's financial crisis. Basically, that poor country's economy is in dire straits and there are pleas for the European Union to write off a crippling debt.

Germany is among the nations firmly opposing this idea.

My Corsican friend Flavie Franceschi, who lives in Boscombe, put a very good status on Facebook the other day. It pointed out that Greece was kind enough to write off a similar debt when the reverse situation occurred in the 1950s as a broken Germany tried to rebuild its economy after the Second World War.

Flavie suggested that maybe Germany could be just as magnanimous now the tables were turned. Well said Flav!

Her comment was historically accurate. At an international conference in London in 1953, the allies – including Greece – agreed to write off more than 50 per cent of West Germany's debt accumulated after the two world wars.

The United States persuaded the European nations to erase part of the debt and relinquish reparations in order to build an economically stable and secure Western Europe as part of an initiative called the Marshall Plan.

July 16 – Wishing a very happy 40th birthday to my great pal Kerry Smith. Have a terrific one, girl!

I've known Kerry for over two decades and regard her as one of the best mates I've ever had. I told her so in a private message on Facebook earlier today.

I've referred to her many times in my books, especially the earlier ones when we were seeing each other on almost a daily basis. We drank together in the Bell, she served me drinks there, we were in a team that did its weekly quiz and we took two holidays and various day excursions together, mostly with others.

Although the youngest adult involved, Kerry was the organiser of a mad, legendary holiday some of the pub's regulars took together in September 1994, staying in a caravan for a week at Haven Holidays' Devon Cliffs site, Sandy Bay near Exmouth.

Detailing it in my first book, *Chronicles of a Lost Soul*, I said it involved the sort of mayhem that would kill you if you tried to keep it up for a year. It was crazy and wonderful. Happy days!

I described Kerry then as 19-going-on-40, such was her wisdom and maturity. I was 41 when I wrote that, but by then she'd helped me sort my head out more than once.

Now she actually is 40. How time flies!

Interestingly enough, she tagged me on Facebook recently when announcing that she was returning to Devon Cliffs – for a no doubt much quieter break!

She did so knowing it would bring back fond recollections of our time there – not only for me, but also for good mates and FB friends Theresa Bevis and Steve Elvidge.

Whatever happens in later life, no-one can ever take away golden memories like that.

Incidentally, birthday greetings also go out to Kelly Millen, a mutual friend of ours.

July 17 – And a happy birthday to Jen Wheeler, aka Dottie, a friendly, bubbly lass who also used to work behind the Bell bar. She's similarly good pals with Kerry.

July 20 – I've lit a candle while remembering Umo, our mate who passed over four years ago today. He was a chatty, amiable guy, mad on Manchester United and motorbikes. Rest easy buddy.

It's really difficult these days, keeping up with all the reports of terrorist attacks across the world. Most are being blamed on violent radical Islamists and several of the most recent ones have taken place in Nigeria – a hotbed of ideological tension.

I say blamed on because how do we know we're being told the truth? I've no doubt that in some cases bloodlust crazies claiming to be Muslims are indeed responsible.

But I'm equally convinced there's a concerted effort to demonize followers of this supposedly peaceful religion in particular and other faiths in general in an evil propaganda war orchestrated by those with their own perverse and brutal agendas.

Why? Who knows? But I'm sure agents provocateur are busy all over the globe causing murder and mayhem while ensuring others are framed then targeted. Politics is a very, very dirty business.

For make no mistake, the perpetrators of these atrocities are political extremists using twisted versions of faiths as an excuse for death and destruction. Muslim, Christian, Jewish – all religious communities find their names equally soiled by these lunatics.

And a lot of the cultural clashes sparking the violence actually stem from tribal conflicts between rival sects of the same religion – deliberately, conveniently and misleadingly being portrayed as Muslims versus Christians by cold manipulators.

I don't doubt that Islamic State is a terrifying reality hell bent on ruthless enforcement of a savage system of government based on an extreme interpretation of that faith.

But I'm increasingly concerned that it's being blamed for just about every terrorist attack in modern times – some I suspect actually the handiwork of unhinged opportunists jumping on this seemingly unstoppable bandwagon.

Or secret service operatives charged with the task of seriously discrediting cultural rivals to the point of framing them for mass murder, stirring up hatred against them.

Meanwhile, Cut Throat Cameron and Barak O'Bomber continue with their mad crusade to pick fights with other countries thousands of miles away, increasingly making us a prime target for terrorist attacks. Thanks a bunch guys!

I thought world statesmen were supposed to act as peacemakers, helping resolve conflicts. Apparently not – especially when millennia-old ideological struggles, ancient vested interests and rich natural reserves are involved.

And we have the fluid, masked and elusive entity of Islamic State the politicians can blame for all the world's problems while doing nothing at all to sort them out – in fact only making matters far worse. Ye gods!

Incidentally, I was reading part of one of David Icke's books the other day and I was struck how, writing over a decade ago, he could predict with such uncanny accuracy recent events and developments on the world stage, especially in the Middle East.

He would no doubt say that he could see it all coming because by then he was realizing what the sinister game plan was and how the shadowy evil elite in charge of things would create and manipulate situations towards its own self-obsessed ends.

Certainly makes you wonder, don't it?

I've already said that I'm pretty sure Icke is right in much of what he claims. But is this nasty network called the Illuminati? I dunno.

Their Internet spokesman says no and in fact they're the good guys fighting to overthrow the dark elite in charge of things. You're probably thinking well he would say that, wouldn't he? – I certainly do.

And even if they're not, I have severe reservations about their cold, clinical and quite stark and brutal vision of the way the world should be run.

As I've said before, I fear it could be used to try and justify a vicious right-wing agenda with fatal or at least severely damaging consequences for many deemed incompatible with its aims and ideals.

I'm part of a growing community of people who think Icke is spot with many of his assertions but who find his remarks about shape-shifting alien reptile rulers, black magic rituals and human sacrifices a bit too bizarre and shocking – a theory too far.

As for his claim about high-powered paedophile rings, well, the wealth of apparent evidence coming to light in the last couple of years or so tends to support this.

And, like him I feel divide and rule is a highly effective tactic widely used to set sections of society with differing world views against each other with devastating consequences while those pulling everyone's strings amass all the wealth and power.

July 21 – The Government's bill that will cut the welfare budget by another £12 billion has been passed in the House of Commons by 308 votes to 124.

This is depressing enough, but what I find absolutely disgraceful is the fact that the Labour leadership ordered the party's 216 MPs to abstain. What?

In the event, 48 of them defied this ruling and voted against. Good on 'em I say – and shame on the abstainers!

This was a golden opportunity for so-called socialists to register their disgust at more right-wing Tory cuts set to hit the worse off. They should have mercilessly ripped in to Cameron's crew in heated debate and then given a resounding no.

But once again we get confirmation that there's little difference between the main parties and they're both determined to slash the welfare bill no matter who suffers.

July 21, mid-evening – I've had a quite wonderful few hours with my very special friend Paula Carruthers at the Bell. Boozing, reminiscing and comparing notes. Cool!

I'm over the moon to be reunited with this gorgeous, crazy and funny lady who will always have a place in my heart.

I deeply love other female pals – and a few close male buddies too – but with her it's different. Paula has her own unique space, somewhere between Joe and Dawn and Shaz, Christine, Carole, Linda, Sam, Kerry, Theresa, Claire, Jen, Bev and Tina W.

I trust that people who know me or have read my books will appreciate why.

July 26 – Went to a super shindig at Sam's yesterday to mark her 40th birthday. It's actually on Tuesday 28th but she chose yesterday for the party as it was a Saturday, more convenient for most people.

Her feller Carl, their two boys Rudy and Bailey and Sam's adult daughter Becca were there plus guests including Bec's dad Russell, her mate Joedie, Jem Hannen, Andy Frend, Rich Jeffery, Sharon Pendleton, Sonia Jamieson and Sam's cousin Diane.

Fortunately the weather was sunny allowing us to spread out in the garden. (Friday it hammered down and today it's raining heavily again.) And a very good time was had by all – alcohol and laughs aplenty.

I've got the BBC TV news channel on in the background and it's telling us that bright people growing up in poorer families are missing out on good jobs that are instead going to less clever individuals from wealthier backgrounds.

This isn't news at all. It's a well-known fact. Tell us something we don't know!

July 28 – Wishing a happy ruby birthday to my very close friend Sam Excell.

I was due to accompany her, Carl and the kids for a celebratory meal at Days – the massive Chinese/English self-service restaurant in central Bournemouth we like a lot and I've mentioned before. But we've had to cancel because Sam has a tummy bug.

This is a great shame and a double whammy, it being her special day and all. We might go later in the week when she's feeling better.

Today is also my pal Steve Elvidge's birthday – nutty Steve, as in that mad Devon holiday back in 1994 which I referred to at some length in my first book, *Chronicles of a Lost Soul/A New Perspective*. Happy birthday mate, have a great one!

July 28 – several hours later – I'm currently re-reading my copy of David Icke's book, *Tales from the Time Loop*, published in 2003.

It's both intriguing and very disturbing to realize how spot-on and prophetic his words have proven to be in light of events in the world since then.

He gave us a potted history of tribal, ideological bloodline struggles stretching over millennia of human existence as a background to what was then going on, especially in the Middle East. Reading it again now makes it even more relevant and shocking.

Icke pulled no punches in describing in graphic detail the mass murder and brutal butchery inflicted upon the Arab countries in general and Muslims in particular that had left colossal bloodstains on many centuries of so-called civilisation.

Cold-hearts in positions of great power and influence were constantly pulling everyone's strings, causing resentment, division and wars while they cleaned up.

They were progressively tightening their grip on the world's wealth and the means to further control and exploit the rest of us.

He said it was still going on in Iraq, Afghanistan and Palestine in the 21st century. And he pointed the finger firmly at the United States and Britain.

Re-reading his book gave me proper food for thought. The numerous accounts of icy, calculated, unimaginable extermination and savagery, indiscriminate mass destruction and deeply humiliating total disrespect made me wonder.

Is it possible that the rise in support for the ruthlessly radical Islamic State among young Brits and others is at least partly a backlash against such atrocious treatment?

Or maybe persecution of Muslims in this country?

A bit of both, I'd suggest. But whether or not that's true, I would implore all concerned to step back and think for a minute – is tit-for-tat the answer?

Of course it isn't – it simply prolongs the agony and misery. Someone's got to draw a line somewhere sometime real soon.

Because there's never a justification for bloodlust violence – no matter how severe the provocation. My heart aches for the casualties on all sides of such bitter disputes.

****

CHAPTER FOUR – SQUADDIES

July 29 – I haven't always been too flattering in my references to the police. Or our armed forces personnel.

I commented in a previous book that some of the biggest thugs and bullies I encountered as a timid boy ended up joining the force or the services.

Earlier in this volume I spoke of right-wing governments sending in the cops to crush dissent by "cracking skulls and smashing up mobile homes."

And I've previously alluded to tightly-wound squaddies marching into Middle Eastern towns and villages "shooting everything that moves."

Numerous other mentions of the forces and the force might well have given the impression I was having a go at all operatives in both. I most certainly was not!

Such behaviour in no way signifies or typifies your average decent bobby on the beat or well-intentioned army private.

I firmly believe that in both cases we're seeing evidence of a force-within-a-force. A hidden division of specially-trained fighters, most of them battle-hardened.

These ruthless individuals mingle with the rank-and-file, frequently stirring them up.

The thoroughly decent and not at all stupid police officers and service folk become brainwashed and controlled by these skilled manipulators who coax them into taking part in savage attacks on innocents. Some unfortunates just go crazy with the stress.

Come to think of it, this pretty much mirrors many similar scenarios in diverse other areas of human existence.

July 31 – Well, we did indeed hold Sam's belated birthday celebration yesterday as she was feeling a lot brighter. She told me she cried for hours on Tuesday, she was so upset that a dodgy stomach had ruined her special day.

We went to Days and then rendezvoused back at hers later for drinkies and silliness. Good it was too.

August 2, evening – Traffic chaos has hit Kent as holiday makers and commercial trucks have been caught up in ridiculously long tailbacks blamed largely on migrants.

Hordes of refugees from violent conflicts in Somalia, Sudan, Eritrea and Syria have fled for their lives to Europe, seen as a safe haven. Thousands of them have ended up in France, bringing to a standstill movement through the Channel Tunnel as a sizeable number of them try to move on to the UK.

It's come at the height of the holiday season and the situation is intolerable. But there are those who claim that the congestion is not all down to the migrants. I tend to agree and I see these unfortunates as convenient scapegoats for politicians eager to look like they're grasping the nettle of an immigration crisis they've created.

My deep concern over the sheer volumes of people flocking to our shores is well documented. But these desperate refugees need shelter and a humanitarian response. European leaders should work together in urgently tackling this growing problem.

Having said that, I've no doubt that the migrant catastrophe has provided a handy cover for others who aren't in such dire straits but who are just as keen to get into our country, some with ill intent.

It's a screwed up old world for sure!

Turning from crisis to sadness, the nation has been rocked by the death of TV legend and family favourite Cilla Black. She passed away in Spain, apparently from natural causes. She was 72.

Tributes have poured in for the Liverpudlian star hailed as a national treasure. Her career spanned more than 50 years as she progressed from chart-topping pop singer to presenter of highly successful family shows *Surprise Surprise* and *Blind Date.*

For people of my generation Cilla was a big part of our growing up and she will be massively missed. As a mate of mine put it so eloquently on Facebook – Ta ra chuck.

In other news, Arsenal beat Chelsea 1-0 this afternoon to lift the Community Shield.

But Chelsea ladies beat Notts County by the same score line yesterday to win the Women's FA Cup in the first final of the tournament to be staged at Wembley.

The Premier League season starts next Saturday and AFC Bournemouth's first match is a home tie against Aston Villa.

August 4, evening – Just had another great afternoon at the Bell with Paula Carruthers. God I love that woman!

We positively revel in our times together; we're totally at ease with each other and we laugh a lot. There's mutual respect and affection and a deep soul connection undiminished by our years apart. And we have that rare, magical ingredient only present in the very best of relationships – we understand each other. And you can't put a price on that!

We've pledged to continue hooking up regularly and never, ever lose contact again. We're the closest of pals for life – always have been, despite the long separation.

I'm feeling elated, strangely liberated and more bloody alive than I have done for years. Sure I've been happy enough in recent times but it's as if at long last I can dare to dream again. Thanks Paula – you're a tonic and a star!

Meeting at the Bell meant we saw our mutual friend dating back to the nineties Paul Savage – the pub's new chef – plus guv'nors Laura and Mark, barmaid Nicola and my mate Ben Avill.

August 6 – It was 70 years ago today that the allies still fighting the Second World War dropped an atomic bomb on Hiroshima, Japan, killing over 100,000 people. Three days later, on the 9th, they dropped a second bomb on Nagasaki in the same country, killing tens of thousands more.

Germany had already chucked in the towel to end the six-year war in Europe three months earlier but the Japanese had refused to follow suit and carried on battling.

But these two bombs had the desired effect – the terrified and traumatised nation surrendered the following week, finally ending the global conflict. Figures for the casualties are imprecise because radiation from the bombs caused many more deaths and injuries as the days, weeks, months and even years unfolded.

As the modern world copes with terrorism, viciously aggressive regimes and blood-drenched ideological clashes, it's both pertinent and poignant to note that to date these are the only times in history that nuclear bombs have been dropped on a country.

And America and Britain were at the forefront of the development and employment of these devastating weapons of mass destruction. Certainly makes you think, don't it?

Ever the optimist, I always hope such anniversaries might serve to make people acutely aware of how seriously damaging conflict can be if it gets out of hand and to pledge to ensure steps are taken to end the friction and injustices that lead to war.

In domestic news, the Labour leadership tussle is heating up following Ed Miliband's resignation immediately after the party failed to win May's general election.

Candidate Andy Burnham, Shadow Health Secretary, says he'll scrap tuition fees, renationalise the railways and introduce a living wage for all ages if he wins power. These are among the policies as he unveiled his personal manifesto today. They're seen as a bid to stave off a strong challenge from left-winger Jeremy Corbyn, who's winning a lot of support from unions and anti-austerity socialists.

Yvette Cooper and Liz Kendall are the other two in the contest, the result of which will be announced next month.

Although not a big fan of Labour – I'm a Green – I welcome any moves to push the party to the left of the political spectrum because it would give voters a proper alternative to harsh right-wing Tory policies.

Under Blair, Brown and Miliband, it was becoming increasingly hard to tell the red rosette crowd from their blue rosette rivals. They waged wars for seriously dodgy reasons and disgracefully backed austerity, merely tinkering with the semantics of it.

No wonder Miliband lost the election – he seemed a decent enough guy with his heart in the right place, but in many ways he resembled a David Cameron wannabe – minus the charisma.

Many will say that Blair only won and held on to power because he moved the party to the centre ground after years of being in the wilderness. I can't argue with this. But that was before Cameron and crew got into Downing Street by default and started inflicting their cruel right-wing policies on a shocked nation.

Labour under Miliband failed to produce a clear, equally radical rival alternative – so come last May's election people were thinking that at least the Tories appeared to know what their policies and plans were so represented the lesser of two evils.

As a Green party member, I think it's so sad that voters can be that negative and defeatist. Nothing will ever change unless they have the courage of their convictions and choose the party they really want in power rather than the one they think will win.

The more folk that do this, the more likely it becomes that things will eventually start to change. The Greens are proving it and gaining ground. So are UKIP and the SNP.

All three are winning support by putting forward bold policies decisively challenging austerity and right-wing Conservative rule. Labour should learn from them.

The Liberal Democrats in the meantime are licking their wounds and trying to salvage at least a small part of their severely damaged reputation. Nick Clegg quit the leadership after the party's well deserved mauling at the election. Coming back's gonna be tough and I don't envy new main man Tim Farron at all.

I've got the BBC television news channel on in the background and it's just been announced that actor George Cole has died.

He had a long and distinguished career spanning seven decades but will probably best be remembered for his portrayal of Cockney wheeler-dealer Arthur Daley in the classic TV comedy-drama series *Minder* with Dennis Waterman. He also starred in a number of St Trinian's films as shady businessman Flash Harry.

Agent Derek Webster said Cole, 90, died at the Royal Berkshire hospital following a short illness, surrounded by his family.

In a much lighter vein, I'd like to wish a very happy birthday to my mate Kevin Sansom – Big Sam – a pal I used to drink with in the Bell and White Horse pubs.

August 7 – And happy birthday today to my friend Tina Wilkins, another former Bell buddy who moved away to Cheshire a while ago but comes back occasionally because her son still lives in Southbourne.

August 9, tea time – I've had a super time today. Phil and Emily came over with Lucas and Chloe.

We had coffee and a catch-up at mine while the children watched kids' TV and generally made themselves at home. Then we took a stroll through Fisherman's Walk so they could terrorize the squirrels, pigeons and fish – ha ha!

Getting to the cliff top, we ate ice creams from the kiosk in the bright sunshine before heading back. More harassment of wild life ensued as we returned to mine, where we parted company as they went to pick up Harvey from Em's mum, Gail.

I love seeing those guys. It's the icing on life's cake for this happy father and grandfather. Absolutely spiffing!

August 10 – Yesterday evening finished off a grand day very nicely indeed – I went to the Bell for landlady Laura Williams' birthday bash. The atmosphere was superb and Laura brought the house down with her impressive version of an Eminem song during the pub's weekly karaoke.

She's actually 22 tomorrow (Tuesday 11th) but she and her feller Mark Evans, the landlord, are going away for a couple of days so the shindig was held last night.

I chatted to both of them and also my mates Paul Savage, John Palmer, John Gaynor, Matt Brant and his lovely lady Dani Knight.

Kelly Adams, Sam and Dave Lowney, DJ Ross Maslin and my friend and close neighbour Billy Clarkson were also there. It's super to see so many friendly faces in my local pub!

August 11 – Happy birthday Laura! Have a great short break away. You've both more than deserved it with the way you've revived my beloved Bell.

****

CHAPTER FIVE
CRAZY TALK ABOUT REPTILES

August 12 – My lyrical muse seems to have deserted me again, at least for now. I've had no new ideas of late and I've run out of old song words I can refurbish and get published. So I guess I'll just have to continue with my dippy prose prattling.

I've often referred to our political masters as cold-blooded. I've even called them reptiles at times – vivid language used to make a point, not to be taken too literally.

But dear old David Icke would insist this is precisely what they are – shape shifting lizard-like aliens hidden in human form, bent on world domination in a global version of Nazi Germany.

He claims that they have a different DNA to the rest of us, which is why they seem completely ruthless and totally devoid of normal human warmth and compassion. And they've been running the show for aeons via history's great empires, he adds.

I've previously told how I go along with much of what he says. It certainly explains a lot, especially our leaders' apparent lack of care and consideration for others' welfare.

I would accept the separate DNA argument as a possible explanation. And I'm sure he's right when he points to ancient family bloodlines being at the heart of millennia-old power struggles still rumbling on today in Iraq, Syria and other trouble spots.

I certainly concur with his view that conventional reality is being run by skilled manipulators using us as little more than disposable assets – cannon fodder, slaves to their savage vision of a world where they have most of the wealth and all the power.

I've often asked the question – why do our overlords insist on prolonging the bloodshed and misery rather than working to achieve parity and peace?

Their attitudes seem so frigging insane to me. Icke's assertions could go a long way to shedding light on this puzzling, tragic and exceedingly frustrating state of affairs.

But reptilian aliens disguised as Royals and other leaders indulging in cannibalism, blood-drinking and human sacrifices? I'm in no position to rule this out completely but it does seem a shade too crazy and weird even for me.

Icke cites the Illuminati as key players in this ages-old ongoing nightmare. But the internet web page bloke claiming to be their spokesman says no, he's got it wrong – they're the good guys fighting to overthrow the evil network he's correctly described.

He also pooh-poohs Icke's lizard alien angle, calling it outrageous nonsense.

Meanwhile, Michael G Reccia, the feller responsible for the Joseph Communication books, appears to debunk any notions of crossovers between Homo sapiens and other species, along with the rest of Darwin's evolution theory.

He claims we're beings of light and energy that turned human ages ago, much, much earlier in our conventional timeframe than scientists have estimated. And he says the environment, natural world, all animals and alien life forms were created separately.

Me? I dunno. I find all these theories fascinating and I dismiss nothing. I keep an open mind at all times as I continue my search for truth.

Ditching any possible explanations just because they seem outlandish and too far removed from our consensus reality means running a real risk of missing vital information that could put us further on the road to enlightenment.

It also plays right into the hands of the manipulators who much prefer to deal with closed-minded people with fixed ideas – they're much easier to influence and control.

And leaving the decidedly bizarre extraterrestrial lizards theory aside for a moment, I'm pretty certain that some very nasty people with self-centred, callous agendas have occupied top positions in politics, banking, business, the military, the legal profession, education, show business and the world's major religions for a very long time.

They've co-operated with each other to amass power and wealth and are thoroughly corrupt. The right connections are crucial and elite bloodlines are probably involved.

In the case of the world's major faiths, inner networks have beavered away tirelessly in secret to twist and embellish divine truth for extremely dubious human purposes, causing friction and bloodshed for millennia.

Millions of sincere followers of the great religions have been blissfully unaware of this, believing everything their priests and ministers have told them whether it's actually backed up by holy texts or not.

And those texts themselves, held up as the words of deities, have been perverted by centuries of mistranslation, edits, deletions and political propaganda.

I'm also of the opinion that Y'shua bar Yosef (the true name of Jesus Christ) was killed because he was a rebel, a revolutionary and reformer who rejected the exalted, privileged position he was born into and groomed for within this deeply shady set-up.

He tried to usher in a more compassionate and caring regime, as described in the words attributed to him in the gospels. He posed a real threat to some so had to die.

All this went far beyond Judaism, local politics and the Roman Empire – these were just tools used to implement the despicable hidden agendas of the unscrupulous.

The virgin birth and resurrection were, I feel, deep symbolism, wrongly accepted as literal fact in defiance of all logic and reason. He was a human being, but one touched by a divinity that coursed through his soul.

All the "God's only begotten son" stuff was vivid picture language intended to indicate his high-ranking birth. But it was deliberately exaggerated to make him sound unearthly and the only messenger of divine truth worth listening to – a politically-charged slap in the face for followers of other belief systems.

He was no humble carpenter but actually a well-connected member of a chosen elite.

And I've little doubt that Y'shua was an enlightened master, a priest-king well versed in the ancient mysteries – including magic. The big difference was that he used his skills and wisdom to promote goodness where others did so to benefit themselves.

Certain scholars say the Bible stories are based on earlier accounts of characters in ancient Sumerian texts, such are the striking similarities.

Or was Y'shua, or Jesus, just a code name, a collective term for a positive vibration that entered the Middle Eastern melting pot of ideological struggle all those centuries ago in a bid to light the way to a more caring and harmonious future?

Both are possibilities of course and no-one knows for sure – but I tend to think he did exist – though not always as portrayed in the scriptures. And I feel his message of peace and harmony is as vital now as it ever was – probably more so.

Some claim he did not die on the cross but survived to marry Mary Magdalene and father children, continuing a royal bloodline dynasty that continues to this day.

But regardless of what happened after the crucifixion, one thing's obvious – in the 2,000 years between then and now, many extra details have been added to the narrative. That's why it's so difficult to find the truth in a welter of conflicting ideas.

The same no doubt applies to other faiths and ideologies. And the brutal divide and rule merchants use the confusion to stir up trouble, causing disputes and wars.

It's a recurring theme throughout human history. And that's why it's so very important to keep an open mind.

These are my views today – August 12, 2015. But I reserve the right to alter them at any time if new information comes to light forcing me to rethink my stance.

There's too much dogma in this world – far too many people with rigid paradigms refusing stubbornly to consider other alternatives.

Free your mind, sisters and brothers. It can be very liberating and illuminating.

August 13, just before noon – I've just listened to Alice Cooper's excellent album A Fistful of Alice, which features live versions of various gems from this mighty fine hard rocker – including the brilliant ballad he co-wrote called Only Women Bleed.

The first time I heard this song was when Julie Covington's cover of it was released as a single in late 1977 and got into the UK top 20. I liked it a lot and assumed she or another female had written it as it told of a woman's suffering in an abusive marriage.

I was gobsmacked to learn quite a bit later that the lyrics were actually written by a bloke – albeit with a woman's name, just to add to the confusion. I thought – how amazingly sensitive and perceptive. From then on I loved it even more. And him.

Alice's rendition on his live album features guitar hero Slash of Guns'n'Roses fame.

But my very first hearing of Julie's version all those years ago made me think and I wrote a snippet of song lyric giving my response to what I saw as the rather sexist assertion that only women suffer in relationships.

It went:

Heard a song this morning
Lady with the blues
Only women bleed, she sang
Only women lose –
Don't you believe it!

(Martin Money, December 8, 1977)

Please bear in mind that I was under the impression a female had written the words.

That's as far as I got with my lyric. Maybe I'll find a home for it in a set of future song words. But that hasn't happened yet – and it's nearly four decades on!

Incidentally, I saw Julie Covington back in 1971 when she was in the London cast of the religious musical *Godspell* alongside David Essex, Jeremy Irons and Marti Webb.

They were all relatively unknown at the time but a couple of years later Essex starred in the movie *That'll Be the Day* and recorded the self-penned hit single Rock On, which reached number three in the UK charts and kicked off his pop idol career.

Jeremy Irons went on to become a successful actor and Julie and Marti both built reputations as well-respected singers and actresses.

Julie's biggest hit was her take on Don't Cry for Me Argentina, a song from the Rice-Lloyd Webber musical *Evita*. It hit number one in 1976.

Sadly. I've never seen Alice Cooper in the flesh. I would have loved that.

August 14 – You know things are getting pretty bizarre and surreal when you turn on your TV and see an advert featuring a singing cat with a lisp.

And continuing the theme of life's stranger aspects, I saw an intriguing and thought provoking Facebook status the other day. It suggested that some drugs are banned because they provide us with a truer version of the world around us than the one we're usually presented with and accustomed to.

Not only that, it went further, asking if the air we breathe contains a mind-numbing element that certain substances counteract and that's why they've been made illegal.

I've often wondered if the food we eat and water we drink has been doctored to the same ends. And I've questioned in print the logic of outlawing some drugs while permitting – even taxing – the use of two of the most damaging, tobacco and alcohol.

Is it all to do with power? – keeping us dazed and in line so we don't challenge the policies and actions of callous controllers exploiting us for their own purposes?

If that's the case, perhaps the alien lizard rulers argument isn't quite so outlandish after all! (Nervous chuckle).

At this point some readers might well be thinking "off he goes again – silly old duffer. Spouting his unhinged hippy gibberish." But I don't care.

And I'd ask them to consider this – is my quirky slant on things really any less puzzling and scary than yours? Reality has crazy and shocking facets whichever way you look at it.

It's all just a matter of perspective. No-one's is exactly the same as anyone else's. And that's one fact of life we can agree on.

Or to put it another way, before you slate my worldview, put hand on heart and tell me that making a TV advert starring a singing cat with a lisp is the epitome of sanity.

And when it comes to worldviews, these are very much governed by what we choose to believe. This can be greatly influenced by others – through what we see, hear, read or pick up from television and the internet.

The human mind is an amazing powerhouse of energy and intelligence. Or at least it can be when working properly.

Sadly, some people are cerebrally retarded. Others are mentally ill. But even those with so-called normally functioning brains are very susceptible to others' control.

Weak wills can be so very easily led by stronger ones. And those whose wills seem to be made of iron can manipulate at every turn, sometimes causing great devastation.

But people keeping their minds open and receptive to all ideas while fully aware of these dangers are less likely to be hoodwinked and exploited.

For make no mistake, there are certain wicked people in high positions who will constantly get others dancing to their tunes – whether they're reptiles or not.

August 15 – I've had two further thoughts my themes of the last couple of days.

Firstly, regarding the apparently bonkers alien lizard theory, when I consider it further, I can quite easily picture certain obnoxious politicians and other famous faces as flesh-eating monsters. They certainly come across as that cold and vicious to me.

But the Royals? – Like most people, I struggle big time with that part of the argument as it's so far removed from the accepted public perception of these much-loved folk.

I question the monarchy and the elitist system it represents, but I have absolutely nothing against these individuals as people.

Of course it's a possibility – albeit an extremely remote one – but the way certain other famous names speak and behave makes it a shade more plausible in their cases.

Plus, you could say that politicians and celebrities are fair game for such admittedly wild speculation, whereas questioning the characters and motives of the Royal Family is treason, seriously challenging the whole basis of our society and national identity.

And that can be unnerving in the extreme. So we quickly rule it out and ridicule others who even consider it. It's better that way – a lot more comfortable.

My second thought was about mind manipulation and control. Mild forms of both are widespread – part of life – but they each become lethal tools in the hands of the brutal.

We hear terrifying stories of hypnotism, brainwashing, secret experiments, powerful drugs and people being robbed of independent thought and reduced to robot-like status to carry out murder and mayhem. In war time certainly but peace time too.

And on that note, today's the 70th anniversary of Japan's surrender that finally ended the Second World War in which more than 60 million people lost their lives.

August 16 – Apparently former Labour Prime Minister Tony Blair's warned against choosing left-winger Jeremy Corbyn as the party's next leader. There's a surprise!

I say if that warmongering clown's against it, it's probably a very good idea. At least it'll give voters a real choice at the next election between harsh, unfair, punitive Tory policies and a more compassionate, greener and more socially-responsible alternative.

Corbyn's manifesto includes growth not austerity, reducing the (alleged) deficit fairly and a foreign policy that "prioritises justice and assistance."

He also wants more public ownership, a lower welfare bill through investment and growth, action on climate change and a major house-building programme as part of a plan to see decent homes for all in both public and private sectors by 2025.

In addition, he calls for a fully-funded NHS integrated with social care, an end to privatisation in health and more protection at work including the scrapping of zero hours contracts.

Some of these are excellent proposals in my book. But not in Basher Blair's it seems.

His successor as party leader and PM, Gordon Brown, has also joined the fight to halt the seemingly runaway bandwagon as Corbyn steams ahead in the leadership race.

Bumbling Brown says Labour should have a credible economic plan if it wants to stand any chance of winning the next election.

Of course it does, but I find it more than a bit rich for him to be saying it – a guy whose own policies were a wishy-washy version of damaging hard line Tory ones.

I think that's precisely why he lost power and why Ed Miliband failed to win it back. Voters need clear distinctions and real choices, and hard line Conservatism of the kind we've been saddled with demands an equally radical Labour response.

I guess the bottom line is that politicians have to decide whether they want to stand by their principles and maintain their dignity and integrity – or sacrifice them in a quest for power at all costs. Now that's a genuine test of credibility, Mr Brown!

New Labour achieved its purpose – an end to 18 years of Conservative rule – but it did so by moving to the political right and abandoning core socialist principles.

Some will ask what's the use of principles of you can't win power – pointing out that you have to be in government in order to change things for the better.

But I say it's far preferable to get there by having the courage of your convictions and keeping others' respect. And if you don't succeed, keep trying until enough people see that your way is better than your opponents' – or tire of their bad, failed policies.

Much as I prefer Corbyn's ideas to Cameron's, I'm not going to be voting Labour if he becomes leader and fights the next election. I'm a card-carrying Green and proud of it. I hate all that tactical voting, let's-sell-our-souls-for-a-taste-of-the-big-time crap.

Oh dear – I'm doing it again, aren't I? I really must try harder to keep this writing lark in a lighter vein and avoid getting embroiled in political arguments.

But it's so damned difficult to bite my tongue – or stick to typing nice words on my computer keyboard – when irritating dolts make daft and inflammatory statements.

****

CHAPTER SIX – SLIPPERS

August 18 – Wishing happy wedding anniversaries to my sister Carol and hubby David and also my friends Tina and Jeff McNally.

At least 20 people were killed yesterday and more than 120 injured when a bomb blast rocked central Bangkok, Thailand.

No-one has yet claimed responsibility but it was thought to be the handiwork of either a rogue Red Shirt political pressure group section or Malay separatists from the country's Deep South. Either way, it represents a serious escalation in violence there.

In sporting news, AFC Bournemouth – the Cherries – still have no points in their historic first-ever season in England's Premier League.

They lost again last night when they played their second match of the campaign away at Liverpool. Once again they were beaten 1-0, just like when they played Aston Villa at home in their debut top-flight fixture.

The good news is that both were narrow defeats, each match had positive and encouraging spells for Eddie Howe's boys and it's still very early days so there's no need to panic just yet.

In fact Liverpool can count themselves lucky – their goal was permitted even though a player was quite clearly offside. And Bournemouth had a disallowed header.

Let's hope the lads can start winning or at least drawing matches soon. Top priority is to avoid relegation – anything else will be a bonus. Come on fellers – you can do it!

Slough Town are struggling a bit near the bottom of the Evo Stick Southern League after doing quite well last season. Opponents include Poole Town and Weymouth.

There's better news for my other team, Manchester United, who have won both their first two matches. But I repeat it's very early days.

August 18 – several hours later – It's evening time now and I've just had another super afternoon with Paula at the Bell. We met there after she had a Black Sabbath image drawn on her arm at Scribe's Tattoo Parlour across the road from the pub.

Spending time with my sexy, humorous, bonkers soul mate is one of life's great pleasures for your happy narrator. Being reunited with her is unexpected bliss.

Our mate Paul Savage, the pub's chef, was also there, plus guv'nors Laura and Mark, lovely barmaid Nicola, Celtic Nicky and a guy I know from the old Home Guard days called Pete, an amiable feller who's quite harmless but as mad as box of frogs.

I once had a two-hour conversation with him about slippers.

August 19 – A second bomb was let off in Thailand yesterday (Tuesday), but luckily no-one was hurt this time around. Still no group has claimed responsibility for either this blast or Monday's explosion that killed more than 20 people.

Although equally shocking and tragic, at least – for once – a lethal terrorist attack isn't being blamed on Islamic extremists, as all other recent ones seem to have been. And that's weirdly refreshing. But it's still a stark reminder of how sick some folk are.

August 20, 3pm – I've just been watching Cilla Black's funeral, broadcast by the BBC news channel in its entirety live and direct from Liverpool, her birthplace where she will be buried next to her parents. It was very moving.

The service included a Roman Catholic mass reflecting Cilla's faith, and alongside the officiating clergy, others taking part included her sons Robert and Ben and her good friends Sir Cliff Richard, Paul O'Grady, Christopher Biggins and her lifelong pal comedian Jimmy Tarbuck.

All spoke with great emotion and affection for the talented singer and TV presenter who was universally loved and will be sorely missed.

Sir Cliff reminisced and sang a religious song, O'Grady told some funny stories with a tear in his eye, and Tarbuck said "being born a lady is an accident – dying one is an achievement." Quite right.

Liverpool's streets were lined with people and the church was packed with wall-to-wall stars – Baron Andrew Lloyd Webber, Sir Tom Jones, Les Dennis, Lorraine Chase and Carol Vorderman to name just a few.

Everyone spoke of Cilla's love of life and amazing ability to connect with people from all backgrounds. And they said she never forgot her humble roots in a tough working-class neighbourhood.

I must admit I shed a few tears – just like I did almost 10 years ago when I watched the televised funeral of footballing genius George Best, another icon dating back to my childhood. His dazzling skills made me a Manchester United fan at the age of 12.

Isn't it strange how we can cry when a much loved celebrity pops their clogs but when it comes to someone really close to us, a big part of our lives, we can't? – Or at least I can't. The pain's far too great and we're terrified if we start we'll never stop.

Mind you, I'm a soppy sod who weeps at emotional scenes in films and TV dramas. It's as if I find a release for pent-up feelings I can't always unleash when reality bites.

August 21 – Talking of reality, there are different levels of perception – a fact I'm appreciating more and more as I continue my search for the truth about existence.

Level one is the five-sense world we're constantly programmed to accept, the one of flesh and bones, wood, steel, bricks and so on. It includes animals, the environment, the universe as we perceive it, others beyond it and all concepts of time and space.

For some, this is the only floor and there's no stairs or lift.

Others envisage a spiritual realm including the afterlife. As they pass on and ascend to this second level, they see themselves going to Heaven, Hell, the Elysian Fields, Nirvana or whichever resting place their religion tells them they go.

It's a self-fulfilling prophesy, for their consciousness will be so plugged in to this mindset that it will indeed take them to such an apparent destination, final or not.

Atheists, of course, will merely see themselves entering a black hole of nothingness.

Again, some will consider this the top storey but it isn't. It's a truer and more accurate reflection of the ultimate reality, but it still uses ideas such as karma and reincarnation that might return consciousness to this Earthly sphere at some point.

It also uses looser definitions of time and space and is still based on polarities such as good and evil, light and dark, positive and negative and male and female.

But I'm convinced there's a level three, where these polarities melt away along with all perceptions of individuality and isolation. At this point our consciousness returns to its natural state – pure spirit, a droplet rejoining the Great Ocean of existence. This Ocean is Oneness, God, the ultimate reality. Peace, love and complete harmony.

But in fact this whole issue is even more complex than that. We are the Ocean and the Ocean is us. There's no distinction and this is our real nature, our home. Five-sense reality and the spirit realms are both corruptions of this ultimate truth we've forgotten.

This is as far as I've got. There may be other levels above and beyond these. I'm not saying I've at last solved the puzzle and I've grasped the meaning of life – that would be very foolish and arrogant. I'm still learning, still opening my mind to new ideas.

I'm on a fascinating, exhilarating journey of discovery. And it's not over yet, not by a long chalk. I'm fully aware that illusions can be very persistent when reality's being manipulated by the devious highly skilled in smoke and mirror exploitation.

Remember – illusions only have power over you if you believe them to be real.

Phew! – Heavy or what? Time for a bit of mundane chatter methinks. Happy second birthday to Roxanna, daughter of Phil's step-sister Ali. Also to my mate Andy Frend.

On a sadder note, it was nine years ago today that Home Guard legend Jim Excell passed over. I'm off to see my great mate Sam, his daughter, later to have a few drinks in his memory.

Good grief! – is it really a year ago that I wrote a similar entry in volume nine of my journal, *Diamonds and Gold*? It's scary how fast time whizzes by – in this warped illusion of reality. Savour every moment girls and boys for each one counts.

Browsing through some old lyrics I wrote yonks ago, I came across this snippet not developed or used anywhere else:

The dream became a fact became a law
The law became religion, led to war

Dream Fact-Law-Re, Martin Money, March 15, 1980.

And a bit of free-form verse I wrote even earlier:

If I were a rock guitarist
If I could play well
I'd give every ounce
No faking
It would be all me
I would not wear false emotion
Like a mantle

I would feel every note
I would be every note
It would be one hundred percent me
I would wring it all out
All the pain, all the joy,
All the hate, all the love
Until it drained me
And at the end
I would feel so good
Exhausted, but satisfied
The kind of satisfaction
That makes you feel
Nothing else matters

It's only rock and roll
But it's everything to me
Nothing else matters.

If I Were a Rock Guitarist, Martin Money. January 23, 1977

I think that illustrates quite well how passionately I feel about a form of music I love.

August 22 – Had a good booze, memory-swapping and fun session at Sam's yesterday as we marked the anniversary of her dad's passing with a few bevvies.

I knew Jim Excell as a stalwart of the old Home Guard social club in Boscombe.

Apart from Sam, Carl, the boys, Becca and me, others attending were Sam's cousin Diane, her daughter Laura, Bec's mate Joedie Watt and our friend Kelly Millen, back in Bournemouth for a few days for her son Ryan's 21st birthday tomorrow.

Kelly knew Jim, and Ryan and his sister Jade grew up looking upon him as a granddad, the two families are that close.

Kelly, who moved to Doncaster last year, is a lovely lady and it was really nice seeing her again. Sam calls Diane her auntie because she's quite a bit older and helped raise her, so is more like an auntie than a cousin.

August 22 – tea time – I'm pleased as punch – AFC Bournemouth have won their first match in the Premier League. They beat West Ham 4-3 away and Callum Wilson grabbed a hat-trick. Marc Pugh got the other goal.

This brilliant result is history in the making as it's not only the Cherries' first victory in the top flight; it also brought their first goals there and first points. Onwards and upward lads!

August 23 – Oh dear! Seven people died after a jet plane crashed on to a road at the Shoreham Air Show in West Sussex yesterday (Saturday).

This is tragic and especially poignant for us Bournemouth folk as our town also stages its annual air show this weekend.

Last night I went to the Bell for Ryan Millen's 21st birthday party. His mum Kelly, dad Brian and sister Jade were there, plus Becca, Alex, Kelly Adams and her guy Matt and some of Ryan's other mates. I also saw guv'nors Laura and Mark and my pals John Gaynor, Lee Robertson and Billy Clarkson.

August 24 – The death toll of the Shoreham Air Show disaster has reached 11 and the authorities fear it could rise to about 20.

A Hawker Hunter jet crashed on to the A27 dual carriageway road while participating in an aerial display on Saturday. It ploughed into cars and exploded in flames.

Emergency services clearing the wreckage say more bodies might well be found. The pilot survived but is in a critical condition in hospital. The future of this and other air shows – including Bournemouth's – are in doubt amid growing concern about their safety.

August 26 – Wishing a very happy birthday to Claire Kimber, my drinking buddy from the old Bell days when she ran the bar for much of Lou and Trudy's time there.

I've just sent Claire a text toasting her personal anniversary and inviting her to a 1990s reunion evening at the pub on Friday

September 11. It was Paula's idea and Kerry, John Gaynor, Paul Savage and Dave "Spoon" Perry have already confirmed. Others have been invited and it should be a good evening of memories and laughter.

Meanwhile, Paula has decided to leave her feller of 13 years or so and move back to Boscombe from the flat they've shared at West Moors the other side of Ferndown. She's not been happy for a while and has now gained the confidence to break away.

Getting out and about with supportive female mates, going on Facebook and restoring contact with old friends from her past – including me – have strengthened her resolve.

I've been playing quite a lot of Genesis music over the past couple of days. I love this band, my sixth favourite ever behind the Beatles, Led Zeppelin, Pink Floyd, the Who and the Rolling Stones.

Their album, Selling England by the Pound, is in my all-time top 20 and they've come up with loads of excellent rock songs – from witty and catchy singles like Jesus He Knows Me, Tell Me Why and That's All to the sublime beauty of Many Too Many, Afterglow, Entangled and After the Ordeal and the surreal epic Supper's Ready.

I could go on – Firth of Fifth, The Musical Box, Invisible Touch, Follow You Follow Me, Land of Confusion, Mama, In Too Deep, Hairless Heart, I Know What I Like, A Trick of the Tail, the Cinema Show – they've laid down so many brilliant tracks.

August 27 – *Sunshine and Ice Volume Two, Descent into Darkness/Déjà vu* has been out two years today. Still waiting for my first royalty cheque, will have to chase up my publishers I guess.

August 28 – Hundreds more migrants are feared dead after two boats sank off Libya yesterday.

And police in Austria say the bodies of 71 people, thought to be migrants, were found in an abandoned lorry found on a motorway, also yesterday.

People traffickers seem to be savagely exploiting poor desperate souls, leading to many of the deaths.

The latest boating tragedy brings the death toll to almost 2,500 so far this year as refugees flee Middle Eastern and African trouble spots only to perish trying to cross the Mediterranean to Europe.

The first vessel, which capsized early yesterday, had nearly 50 people on board. The second, carrying about 400 passengers, went down later.

It's believed that about 200 people were rescued but concerns mount as the search continues for the missing. Unconfirmed reports say the refugees came from Syria, Bangladesh and several sub-Saharan African countries.

Meanwhile, the bodies of 59 men, 8 women and four children were found in the Austrian truck incident. Police said these victims also appeared to be Syrians and probably died after suffocating in the vehicle.

Three people, thought to be Bulgarian, have been detained in Hungary. They are suspected of dumping the lorry after their trafficking attempt went tragically wrong. Police sent to investigate the abandoned vehicle on the A4 motorway towards Vienna discovered the decomposing bodies yesterday morning.

Blimey! – This whole migrant crisis is getting way out of hand. In recent times, more than 100,000 have landed in Italy, whilst another 160,000 have crossed to Greece.

Germany, France and the UK are the planned destinations for many of them and we've seen chaos both sides of the Channel Tunnel this summer.

Top politicians in Europe really do have to work together urgently to tackle this growing problem as migration and immigration become the focus of much anxiety across the continent.

Yes, our leaders should be exercising better control over the huge numbers of people flocking to our shores – but at the same time they should recognize the massive difference between those just wanting a better lifestyle and terrified folk fleeing battle zones in fear of their safety.

I'd suggest an immediate review of foreign policies is also needed as bombing campaigns continue in the Middle East, aggravating the problems.

As pioneering microbiologist Louis Pasteur once said: "One does not ask of one who suffers: What is your country and what is your religion? One merely says: You suffer, that is enough for me."

August 29, 5pm – I was at the Royal Bournemouth Hospital this afternoon visiting my pal Andy Frend, who's just had some devastating news – he's terminally ill.

He has cancer of the lungs too advanced for surgery and it's rapidly spread to his brain.

This is a huge shock for Andy and everyone who knows him. We shared a drink and a laugh just a month ago at Sam Excell's 40th birthday party. And he's only 51 – it was his birthday eight days ago.

Largely lost for words, I came up with a feeble joke, telling him that if he'd wanted to date a nurse there were easier ways of going about it.

I guessed it would appeal to his sense of humour – and luckily I was right. He smiled. I mean, what can you say in such circumstances? – It doesn't much matter really. You just have to show up and let the ill person know they have your support.

As I left, he called to me and gave me the thumbs up. Moving, tragic, heart-breaking.

Andy will be sent home soon with medication and a care team on hand to ease his suffering. Sadly, that's all they can do for him. It's only a matter of time – and not much time at that.

The whistle's just gone to end AFC Bournemouth's home tie against Leicester, a 1-1 draw that keeps the Cherries mid-table in the Premier League after four matches.

August 30 – Today is my great buddy Jem Hannen's 51st birthday. I wish him all the best but Andy's plight will have taken the shine off it for him as they're close mates.

Home Secretary Theresa May was on the news this morning saying freedom of movement within the EU should be the freedom to move to a job, not switch to another country and then seek work or welfare benefits.

I agree – surely that's just plain old-fashioned common sense? After all, English people ensure they have work and accommodation sorted before emigrating, don't they? If not, they're bloody fools!

But once again I make the crucial distinction between economic migrants and refugees fleeing trouble spots in fear of their lives – especially when our governments' foreign policies have helped create such violent clashes.

September 2 – It's birthdays galore at the moment! Today it's my mate Rod Marlow's 50th and yesterday was my old Bell drinking pal Paul Dangerfield's 49th.

Today is also Jack Hannen's 24th – Jack being Tony's son, Jem's nephew. I've sent Rod, Paul and Jack Facebook messages, but in all their cases, as in Jem's three days ago, any celebrations will be tinged with sadness over Andy's dire situation.

September 2, 9pm – Just had a terrific time at the Bell with the quite stupendous Paula Carruthers. It got a bit emotional at times as the link between us is unbreakable and the deep love we share without question.

She's moving from West Moors to Springbourne – an area of Bournemouth just the other side of Boscombe – on September 26. It'll be great having her living so close again, meaning we'll be able to see each other more often.

Actually, it'll be more than great – it'll be wonderful!

I have so much admiration for her, taking such a brave step – uprooting herself from a failed 13-year-old relationship and basically starting over. Well, home arrangement wise anyway. She's keeping her job at Tescos in Ferndown as she's got a car so can drive there and back.

September 4, 11am – It's been quite a morning and I've been moist-eyed for two reasons, one very bad and the other very good.

The bad aspect was hearing of Andy's demise. Facebook is full of tributes to him. Farewell friend and thanks for all the fun times.

It's a massive shock to everyone who knows him as it all happened so fast. It's hard to believe I was having a beer and a laugh with him just a few shorts weeks ago.

The good but equally emotional feature of my morning was a video link Paula had sent me through Facebook of a Shania Twain song called From This Moment On.

Listening to the lyrics gave me one of those "wow" moments and yes, I got more than a bit misty-eyed. Check them out and you'll see what I mean.

The fact that it came within minutes of learning about Andy only intensified the experience. Tears of sadness, tears of joy – the two extremes of life.

September 5, 1am – Can't sleep. So much running through my mind after an exceptionally heart-tugging day.

Cut up big time over Andy, I needed my mates. And they came through for me. Big time. As I knew they would.

Sam had already invited me to hers before we knew of our mate's demise. So I went to see her and Carl this (now yesterday) afternoon and we had a few drinks in Andy's memory, joined by Tina Mcauley, Russell Hall and Sam's rellies Diane and Laura.

That was great and helped me through the day. No doubt it applied in reverse, because Sam, Carl Russ and Tina were all Andy's mates too. But not as close as our mutual pal Rich Jeffrey. We all really feel for him because he and Andy were like brothers.

Tons of others will miss him too – far too many to mention. He was a guy loved by some and liked by a heck of a lot. It's a legacy we all aspire to – respect buddy, RIP.

And on a purely personal note, I had many great times with Andy. Boozing, partying and laughing a lot. I'll never, ever forget that last and oh so poignant thumbs up.

Much as though Sam and company lifted my spirits, it's Paula I have to thank the most. It was her Shania Twain Facebook link that hit me within minutes of learning of Andy's passing – and got me weeping tears of joy as well as sadness.

And some of the stuff she's been saying to me today via private FB messages has been pretty bloody awesome too. Just when I needed it most. Fate or what?

A LOVE STORY

They met, became friends in an instant and established a strong bond – but neither of them realized quite how strong back then.

They lost contact and as the months turned to years they put each other to the back of their respective minds. But they kept the love and never forgot – mentioning each other to their peers frequently as the memories resurfaced.

Almost two decades later, by a strange and wonderful quirk of fate, they met again. And it was like all those years were wiped out in a flash.

But it was different second time around. And so much better. Older and wiser, they both appreciated far more fully what they'd had in their grasp but failed to hold on to.

Reunited, they decided that this time they'd get it right. They were soul mates who loved each other very much. They felt so comfortable together, they understood and respected each other and they laughed a lot.

At the end of the day, that's what it's all about, isn't it?

Love is the answer.

THE END.

September 5, evening – I've just watched England's footballers thrash San Marino 6-0 to qualify for next year's Euros with three group matches still to go.

Theo Walcott got two but skipper Wayne Rooney was the star, putting away a penalty kick to open our account while making history as England's joint top scorer ever with 49 goals, equalling Sir Bobby Charlton's record.

Well done lads!

Blimey! – David Cameron's once again taken me by surprise by coming out with something I actually agree with.

He's been on the news basically saying we should help ease the refugee crisis by going direct to the root of the problem – the countries involved.

He wanted us as a nation to take people straight from the emergency camps in Syria, Afghanistan and other flashpoint lands and transfer them to safe havens in the UK – while assisting such strife-torn countries to find peaceful solutions to their troubles.

This was a far better option than taking more and more people from Europe, where the refugee and migrant crises had become hopelessly confused, he said.

Sounds good to me, but as ever with this guy I seriously question the motives behind the rhetoric. Especially when we're getting renewed calls for military intervention in Syria as a means to sorting out its bloodstained mess.

For some, this has been the game plan all along and the mass evacuation of desperate families is a great chance to implement it while using the flimsy justification that we're acting in the petrified inhabitants' interests.

Makes me wonder whether this is vicious opportunism or coldly calculated design.

Just like with 911 and other atrocities drawing aggressive, warrior responses.

Are such shocking, violent and tragic events engineered to manipulate us into backing wicked agendas? David Icke and others would say a resounding yes and I must admit I'm becoming increasingly persuaded they're right.

Wacky conspiracy theory? Maybe, but it's appearing ever-more plausible to this deeply worried observer. Often it's the only explanation that makes any sense.

I believe it's no coincidence that we've already invaded Afghanistan in recent times and the pressure's growing for us to send the troops into Syria as well.

Meanwhile, young Muslims continue to be radicalised in our own country. Ye Gods!

As tensions mount all round, I'm feeling more and more like Alice in Wonderland, where nothing was quite as it seemed.

****

CHAPTER SEVEN – A TERRIFIC ADVENTURE

September 6, evening – Just had a brilliant day that lifted my spirits no end. It wasn't planned but sometimes the best ones aren't.

Paula contacted me to ask if she could come over as she was at a loose end. Sure, I said, so she did.

We had coffee, a chat and a laugh at my flat then strolled in the sunshine through Fisherman's Walk to the cliff top, where we talked and wise cracked overlooking the sea for a while before adjourning to the nearby Commodore Hotel for a meal.

Then we walked back, had another coffee at mine and chin wagged and joked a bit more before she left to drive home.

I love every moment I spend with her. And she appreciated the chance to escape a domestic situation that's becoming intolerable pending her move to Springbourne.

September 9 – And another few super hours basking in her company. We met at the Bell again yesterday after she'd clinched the deal for the flat she's going to rent.

Having checked with her, I went public about our renewed relationship on Facebook yesterday evening – and I was overwhelmed by the number of lovely comments I got.

Phil, Emily and loads of friends said some really nice things. I went back to Paula saying I hoped I hadn't embarrassed her or made her feel under any pressure. She assured me it was fine.

After all, she's just leaving one 13-year-old withered relationship and the last thing she needs right now is to plunge head first into another heavy duty alliance.

We've decided to take it slow and easy but we're both as excited as love-struck teenagers. This is going to be very interesting indeed and is already quite exceptional.

But then again, how do you define a relationship? It's a word bandied about a lot and means different things to different people.

I have relationships with all sorts of folk including my dentist, my landlord and my friend's pet dog.

Of course, the word relationship is usually accepted to indicate two people being a couple. But even then, what does this mean?

Some couples are married and live together. Others live together and are engaged with a view to getting wed at some point – or maybe not, being happy to keep it like that while letting others know they're unavailable.

Many couples don't live together but have their own homes and retain a degree of independence – and it's looking like we're going to be like that, which suits us both fine. At least for the foreseeable.

One thing's for sure, though – this is the start of a terrific adventure for both of us. Who knows how it will go? It will be fun finding out!

History's being made all over the place. Last night Wayne Rooney netted a penalty kick to become England's top goal scorer of all time with 50 – one ahead of Sir Bobby Charlton.

Rooney's goal came as Roy's boys beat Switzerland 2-0 at Wembley to keep up their 100 per cent match-winning record in the qualifying ties for Euro 2016.

And today the Queen becomes our longest-reigning monarch ever, beating the record set by Victoria – 63 years and 216 days.

Meanwhile, the refugee and migrant crises and the fast-deteriorating situation in the Middle East are making some people ask if World War Three is imminent.

Let's hope not, but I must admit that very thought has crossed my mind more than once in recent weeks as I've watched the TV news with growing anxiety.

September 11 – It's fourteen years ago today that bloodlust crazies rammed planes into buildings and unleashed a horrifying nightmare that's getting worse by the day.

I've lit a candle and put a short tribute on Facebook for the 3,000 or so victims, their families and loved ones.

Whoever was responsible – and opinions vary – the resultant attacks and counter-attacks since then, the wars and terrorist atrocities, the rising tension in the Middle East and its accompanying migrant and refugee crises all seem to be precursors of a global catastrophe, possibly a Third World War.

But in my little corner of existence, things are looking very good indeed thanks to the lovely Paula. Watch this space!

September 12 – I'm over the moon at the moment. Paula came over yesterday tea-time as we'd planned a nineties reunion evening at the Bell for some of the old crowd.

As it happens, the event was a bit of a damp squib because hardly anyone turned up for it. But we still had a few drinks and a cracking good time and Ross the deejay did us proud, playing classic tunes from that decade throughout the session.

And it was good for Paula to see Paul Savage and John Gaynor again.

She stayed at my flat last night and this morning we took a stroll through Fisherman's Walk to sit on the cliff top for a while before she returned to West Moors lunchtime today. I've fallen in love with her all over again and it's brilliant!

Incidentally, two posts I put on Facebook this week have attracted the two biggest responses I've ever received since joining the site at Christmas 2010. A tribute status to Andy with photo drew 29 likes and the announcement about Paula and me getting together 26 likes and 21 comments. I love my mates!

September 13 – Happy birthday Tina Mcauley, my friend I met through Sam Excell.

Well, Jeremy Corbyn is the new face of Labour, having won the party's leadership tussle by a mile. Good – as I keep saying, this gives voters a real and distinct alternative to deeply damaging Tory policies.

Corbyn is the darling of left-wingers, the trade unions and a growing army of new young Labourites who have joined the party since the general election in May.

Doom and gloom merchants are warning that his victory has made Labour unelectable and sentenced it to many years in the wilderness as a wacky fringe party.

Cameron, Osborne and their supporters are no doubt rubbing their hands with glee.

Me? – I'd much rather have Corbyn's clearly more compassionate approach than a continuation of harsh, punitive, unfair and divisive right-wing measures any day.

Ironically, the latter could be exactly what we do end up with as folk avoid Labour like the plague every time they're called upon to vote. That's both worrying and sad.

But I say who the hell needs New Labour and Brown and Blair's muddled and tired pseudo-Tory, austerity-minded policies anyway? Good riddance to them.

I can imagine leading Greens Caroline Lucas and Natalie Bennett being able to work with Corbyn in ways they would never ever contemplate with Cameron and company.

And I can foresee a Labour revival north of the border, where it was almost obliterated by the Scottish National Party landslide at the general election.

Rats! AFC Bournemouth lost again – 3-1 away at Norwich – so are slipping down the Premier League table again. Come on fellers – another win or two, or even a few draws, would boost confidence no end in your bid to stay up.

September 14 – As David Icke once wrote: "We will travel home in a new reality, not a new Ferrari." Very well put, sir!

September 15 – I've been playing quite a lot of Yes music over the past week or so. I'm listening to the excellent live double CD set called Yessongs at the moment.

I love this band. The show I saw them do at the Empire Pool, Wembley, in 1977 was outstanding – one of the best gigs I've ever been to.

They're my seventh favourite group of all time behind the Beatles, Led Zeppelin, Pink Floyd, the Who, the Rolling Stones and Genesis.

Like all the truly great bands and solo artists, they have that wonderful knack of producing beautiful, powerful music that makes your heart soar and your eyes leak – rock at its very best.

Speaking of which, I went to Boscombe last week to try and find one classic rock live show DVD – and returned with a totally different but equally impressive one.

Having recently played A Fistful of Alice, A CD of live Alice Cooper music, I went to Snu Peas Records second-hand shop to see if they had a DVD of *Welcome to My Nightmare*, a legendary stage show featuring Alice at his best.

Unfortunately, they didn't have it, but as my fingers wandered from the "A" section to the "B" compartment, I came across a DVD of the Band's movie the *Last Waltz*, so I got that instead.

For those who don't know, *The Last Waltz* is a Martin Scorsese film centring on the seminal American group's final performance, staged in San Francisco in 1976.

They decided to go out with a bang so invited some of their mates along to join in – and it turned into a veritable who's who of rock icons, such as Bob Dylan Eric Clapton, Ringo Starr, Ronnie Wood, Neil Young, Joni Mitchell, Muddy Waters, Emmylou Harris, Neil Diamond, Ronnie Hawkins and Van Morrison.

Needless to say, the film is a joy to behold – well worth the fiver I paid for it and a fitting substitute for the one I went out looking for. I'll keep my eyes peeled for Alice's film, which I used to have on video.

Incidentally, while at Snu Peas I also acquired CDs of Kraftwerk, Steve Hillage, Yes, the Eurythmics and Prince, plus the excellent folksy soundtrack album to the superb movie *The Wicker Man*, one of the finest horror thrillers ever made.

September 16 – Yesterday was lovely. Paula came over and we went to see Sam, who was holding a little party for a guy who was 50 last week.

His name's Mick and he's our mate Enoch's brother. They'd both come down from their native Yorkshire to attend a surprise 21st birthday shindig on Saturday (19th) for Sam's son Alex and his best mate Ryan Millen.

You may recall me mentioning Ryan a few pages back when it was actually his big day. It's not Alex's 21st until early October, but Sam and Ryan's mum Kelly decided to split the difference and stage a joint celebration half-way between the two dates.

It was the first time I'd met Mick and it was Paula's first encounter with Sam, Carl and their family and friends. I'm delighted to say Paula enjoyed herself and Sam, her cousin Diane and our mutual friend Tina all told me they liked her.

And I was in my element. Not only did I spend another few wonderful hours with my woman – God, it sounds so good to say that – I also introduced her to some of my mates.

The fact that they got on so well was a terrific bonus – but then, I was pretty sure they would. Sam was so impressed with Paula that she invited us both to spend Christmas Day with her, Carl, Bec and the boys – a very kind gesture no-one makes lightly.

September 18 – I'm playing a CD of the album Electric Ladyland in honour of the late, great Jimi Hendrix, who died 45 years ago today.

The circumstances of his demise are shrouded in mystery and heated debates rage on even now – murder or accidental drug overdose?

Either way, he was only 27 and his passing was a massive loss to the rock music world he'd ignited with his brilliant and astounding guitar playing that could switch from loud and incendiary to soft and melodic in a heartbeat.

American-born Jimi settled in England and set about revolutionising the way people played the instrument.

His mastery of feedback and distortion was incredible and he threw out amazing guitar licks while playing the instrument behind his head. He also used his teeth, set fire to his guitar and used it as a phallus doing pelvic thrusts up against his speakers.

His act often ended with him smashing it to smithereens, and yet he could just as easily sit on a stool with an acoustic and play the sweetest music you've ever heard.

The violent rock and roll rebel stance aside, he was an excellent writer and interpreter of songs with a poetic flair illustrated by his lyrics. He could also be painfully shy.

In short, he was a genius. But he was also a wise thinker with a good heart – a gentle soul with a beautiful spirit.

His electrifying stage shows are the stuff of legend and he blew everyone away with his fantastic performances at the Isle of Wight, Monterey and Woodstock festivals.

Rest in peace, Jimi – the world has been considerably poorer since your departure.

Another brand new lyric has crystallized in my mind. The inspiration should be obvious:

TO THE STARS AND BACK
Martin Money, September 18, 2015

I love you to the stars and back, you brighten up my day
You've made me feel so wonderful, much more than words can say
You lay for hours in my arms, your head upon my chest
We talk and laugh and then make out, this feeling is the best

I never thought I'd get the chance to savour this once more –
The simple joys of sweet embrace and clothing on the floor
I want to kiss you head to toe and make you feel so fine
To please you any way I can, I'm chuffed to bits you're mine

To walk through woodlands, watch the waves and have a drink
*   or three*
And all with someone I adore and who's in love with me
I'd long ago resigned myself to being on my own
So this is such a great surprise, my mind is truly blown

Thank you babe – now I can dream again
Easing all the pain, dancing in the rain
Together forever from now on –
That's the way to go, let our deep love show
It's you and me from now – that truth is plain for all to see

I've had my share of heartbreak, darker times and rotten deals
But now I've hit the jackpot, or at least that's how it feels
I love you to the stars and back, you brighten up my day
You've made me feel so wonderful, much more than words can say

Thank you babe – now I can dream again
Easing all the pain, dancing in the rain
Together for ever from now on –
That's the way to go, let our deep love show
It's you and me from now – that truth is plain for all to see

I love you to the stars and back, you brighten up my day
You've made me feel so wonderful, much more than words can say
I never thought I'd get the chance to savour this once more –
The simple joys of sweet embrace and clothing on the floor

Thank you babe – now I can dream again
Easing all the pain, dancing in the rain
Together forever from now on –
That's the way to go, let our deep love show
It's you and me from now – that truth is plain for all to see.

September 19 – And another one, a bit shorter and simpler:

SHOWER ME WITH LOVE

Martin Money, September 19, 2015

Holding hands, arm in arm or bodies intertwined
Coax my fragile heart to beat, ease my troubled mind

Coz you fit me like a glove, baby,
Fit me like a glove
Fit me like a glove, baby,
Shower me with love

Talking loads, cracking jokes, we put the world to rights
Let 'em have their wars and hate, leave 'em to their fights
We have us, you and I, and we've got all this
Had enough of pain and strife, healing with each kiss

And you fit me like a glove, baby,
Fit me like a glove
Fit me like a glove, baby,
Shower me with love

Holding hands, arm in arm or bodies intertwined
Coax my fragile heart to beat, ease my troubled mind
We have us, you and I, and we've got all this
Had enough of pain and strife, healing with each kiss

Never thought I'd have another chance to feel such bliss

Coz you fit me like a glove, baby,
Fit me like a glove
Fit me like a glove, baby,
Shower me with love.

September 19, tea-time – Yippee! – AFC Bournemouth have won a second Premier League match, pushing them back up the table. They beat Sunderland 2-0 with goals by Callum Wilson and Matt Ritchie.

Their first home win of the season lifts the Cherries to 11th, just below the half-way mark, and they currently sit proudly above last season's champions Chelsea and top teams Liverpool and Tottenham – although in fairness the last two didn't play today.

Keep it up fellers – use this confidence-booster as a springboard for more wins and draws that'll keep you safe from relegation!

September 20 – Wishing a very happy birthday to my friend Tina McNally. Hoping she has a good one.

Last night was excellent – Alex and Ryan's joint 21st celebration was a triumph with loads of people who got on well.

In addition to the birthday boys and their same-age friends, Sam, her mate Kelly (Ryan's mum), Bec, Ryan's sister Jade, Russell, Diane, Laura, Joedie, Tina, Jem, Rich, Sonia, her son Ziggy and her man Steve, our mate Chris Davis, Enoch and Mick, Ryan's dad Brian and Kelly's brother Gary (Ryan's uncle) were also there.

Sam and Kelly had hired a large downstairs room at Mr Green's pub in Boscombe for the private party. It had its own bar and a deejay provided the music. It was great.

But for me personally it could have been even better. Someone very special was missing – my Paula. She wanted to go but couldn't due to her circumstances, which thankfully change next Saturday when she moves a lot closer to us all.

September 21 – Liberal Democrats are currently meeting in Bournemouth for their party's autumn conference. Nick Clegg is speaking live on the telly as I write.

He's talking about a fightback. Sorry mate, it's not going to happen. You lot are finished. You had a golden opportunity and you blew it.

So what's the Oxford English Dictionary definition of a Liberal Democrat?

Well, it's this: "A member of a party (formerly the Social and Liberal Democrats) formed from the Liberal Party and members of the Social Democratic Party."

Hmm. That seems very weak to me. Here's my version – "A traitor, a turncoat, someone who says one thing then does the exact opposite."

Bitter? You bet I am. After years of voting Liberal then Lib Dem, thinking they were decent folk with compassionate and sound policies, I now see these despicable articles for what they are – untrustworthy tossers!

What was it Pete Townsend wrote, and Roger Daltrey sang? – Oh yeah, "won't get fooled again."

I just hope and pray the Greens don't turn out to be just as bad. I'm trusting them to show the rest what politics should be all about – properly looking after people, animals and the environment. It's about bloody time somebody did!

September 22 – Just had another lovely Tuesday with my Paula. It's usually the only guaranteed day of the week she has off from working in Ferndown Tesco's so we make the most of it. We met at the Bell – her choice as she wasn't driving this time.

We had a few pints then adjourned to my flat for several hours before she got a cab back to West Moors – having bussed over this morning. It's 9pm and she's just left.

It was wonderful to spend the day with her. We're both looking forward immensely to next weekend, when she moves to Springbourne meaning we can have a lot more time together. We're both delighted to be reunited after all these years.

In my first book I referred to Paula as a "tart with a heart" – a well used description she actually applied to herself more than once back then, almost two decades ago.

She still has that big heart but the tart bit no longer applies – far from it. In fact it always was a misnomer. In those days she was lost and confused, that's all – sexually active but fuelled by alcohol and a deep-seated anger.

Happily, she's a lot more together now – still sexy, still crazy, still funny but minus the darker aspects that led her into so much trouble. I'm pleased for her and would be even if I wasn't part of the equation. The fact that I am is just a huge bonus for me.

Paula is spirited and strong-minded and in some ways very confident – although that confidence has been battered and undermined over the past decade or so. Now she's regaining it, thank the stars. But in other ways she's self-conscious and self-doubting.

I'm the same. My confidence in my own worth and abilities has reached new heights but I'm self-conscious about my appearance, don't like being out after dark on my own, get nervous in crowds and have a real issue with travelling, even short distances.

We're both walking paradoxes but nowadays we're both more likely to care a lot less about what other people think of us – unless they're dear to us, of course.

We boost each others' confidence, whether it's about physical attributes or life in general. We're at ease and honest with each other and have trust and understanding.

Such things are priceless and sadly missing from so many relationships. That's why they fail. We're both determined to ensure that ours doesn't.

In short, we adore each other, mind and body. How cool is that?

And at the end of the day, physical attraction has bog all to do with physical form. Beauty truly is in the eye of the beholder. You can be drop dead gorgeous but if your nature's ugly you're an ugly person. Only the incredibly shallow would disagree.

We all have our flaws and blemishes. But Paula is beautiful to me.

I've just re-read my two new lyrics written about her. They're among the rudest I've ever written, especially Shower Me with Love. Notice I say rude, not crude, for nothing's overt but much is implied. That's one way to circumvent the censors!

September 23 – Happy autumn equinox folks, and happy birthday to my friend Diana Slater and rock legend Bruce Springsteen.

Yep, today's the first day of autumn and what a beautiful sunny day it is. It's 8.30 am and I think after breakfast I'll saunter through Fisherman's Walk woodlands to sit on the cliff top for a while overlooking the sea before heading back home via the shops.

Hello again, I'm back now. Very nice it was too. The wooded walk was as pleasant as ever and I thoroughly enjoyed passing through the lovely fish pond area on my way to park myself on a wooden bench to enjoy stunning views of the Dorset coastline.

The warm sunshine kissed my face and loads of people strolled by, many of them walking their dogs. Terrific!

This is one of life's great bonuses for someone like me, lucky enough to live 10 minutes away. It's so close at hand and totally free of charge.

Isn't it interesting how some of life's sweetest pleasures are the simplest ones?

And speaking of sweet pleasures, I can't stop thinking about Paula. Who would've thought it? An ageing, reluctant but resigned and contented single guy like me having a girlfriend again after all this time and being head over heels in love once more?

I thought those days were long gone. How chuffed am I to learn they're not? This has all been a joyful surprise to me. I've been knocked sideways in the best way possible.

I feel regenerated, vibrant and young again. Well, young-ish at least. It's ruddy marvellous! Thanks Paula – my lover, my soul mate and yes, my best pal.

I know I said I don't do best friends any more but this is different. It's rare, special and oh so precious. The fact that it's so unexpected intensifies its power. All I can say is – wow! I'm delighted and eternally grateful this amazing lady found me again.

I have mates who can't understand it when people say their love partner is their best friend. As I've already said, it seems the most natural thing in the world to me – the way it should be. Joe and Dawn were both my besties in their days. Now Paula is.

I know some of my peers feel the same way about their lovers. We think there's something missing if this isn't the case. Others are similarly adamant that your partner and your best mate should be two different people. I can't really see why.

What now for Paula and me? Who knows? But whatever it is we're in it together – to the end.

You will notice I've just referred to Joe, Dawn and Paula in the same paragraph. Some folk would chide me for this, seeing it as a total no-no.

Such people also firmly believe that you shouldn't talk about ex-lovers in the presence of current ones. Why not? I can't see the problem.

Okay, if you constantly drone on about a former romantic partner and mention them more than you do the one you're actually with, there's something seriously wrong and you're heading for trouble.

And, of course, you shouldn't constantly draw comparisons – sure, do it once in a while but only if it favours your current love interest.

I talk about Joe to Paula and she talks about her former lovers to me. Neither of us thinks this strange because our relationship is based on trust, honesty and openness.

Let's face it – we both have histories and baggage of all kinds, good and bad. It seems perfectly normal to both of us to accept this, embrace it and discuss it.

I actually speak about Joe quite a lot, to Paula and to other people. She was a big part of my life, at the time I loved her dearly, we went through a lot together and we had our treasured Phil, who in turn has provided us with our wonderful grandchildren.

To not mention her seems just plain weird, especially when I still see her fairly regularly at family gatherings.

And Paula has her son Matthew who's given her one granddaughter with another on the way. For her to omit any references to him, his dad or those children would seem equally peculiar to me.

Sadly, there are the walking wounded whose pasts had such horrendous aspects they've chosen to block them out for self-preservation. I sympathize with them.

But unless this is the case, I really don't get people's reluctance to revisit bygone times. Unless they do it incessantly, which again would indicate that there's something amiss with their current situation.

I guess it all depends on how comfortable and secure you feel in yourself and with each other. Well, that's my view anyway. Others would disagree. C'est la vie.

September 24 – Two days to go now until my lover's back in town. Whoop whoop!

Paula loves her puzzles, especially those online murder mystery thingies. And at the end of the day, life is one big puzzle.

I've had a major piece missing from mine for so long I'd adapted my worldview to compensate. Paula's brought it back. She completes me.

Oh, by the way, I was wrong when I surmised that she'd only just joined Facebook and found me on there shortly afterwards. In fact she's been a member for longer than I have.

It's just that a feller we both know from the good old Bell 90s days has recently started working at Tesco's Ferndown store, where she's been employed for 13 years. The guy's name is Dave "Spoon" Perry and I've mentioned him before.

Anyway, they got talking, realized they knew each other, became Facebook friends and through him she found Theresa and through her, me.

I've completed the circle by become FB friends with Dave, who I must owe several pints as he was the key that initiated our happy reunion.

Paula told me she'd actually blacked out much of that 90s era as it held so many bad memories for her. But seeing Dave again, and then me, has brought back glowing recollections of the better aspects, including our deep connection.

Only now are we both realizing – or rather remembering – just how deep our love for each other has always been. But we both pushed it to the back of our minds, thinking we'd never meet again.

It refused to go away though and nice thoughts about each other resurfaced frequently. This is fate. It's a soul thing. And it's pretty damned spectacular.

On that highest of notes I shall close part one of this book. Part two follows…

****

AMAZING MESSAGES

Part Two

September to December 2015

CHAPTER EIGHT – A FRESH START

September 25 – Well, it's less than 24 hours now until Paula returns to Bournemouth after 13 years living out in the wilds of West Moors.

A new life chapter has started for both of us – a fresh start. And it's so flipping cool!

I love many things about that woman. One of them is the way she accepts me as I am with all my flaws and blemishes. She's doesn't try to change me any more than I do her. And that's important.

You may have noticed that I can't stop referring to my Paula at the moment. I can't stop thinking about her or mentioning her to others either. Or smiling. I feel like the cat that's got the cream. I've not been this happy for years.

But I don't want to bore you or make you feel nauseous with my constant love cloud prattling. So I'll shut up now. After all, the world isn't all sweetness and light. Far from it.

The biggest news story at the moment is the deaths of more than 700 people crushed in a stampede in Saudi Arabia close to Mecca, a city very important to all Muslims.

More than 850 others were injured as two groups of pilgrims collided at the intersection of two narrow streets on Thursday. Panic and chaos ensued.

September 26 – Today's the day Paula and I have been looking to for weeks – she moves a lot closer to me. She's got time off from work but will obviously be a bit busy for the next few hours so I'll be seeing her tomorrow (Sunday).

Yesterday evening was different. Instead of just gathering in her kitchen to drink, chat and have a laugh, Sam decided we should have a games night. So after her boys had gone to bed we sat at a table in the living room – their domain during the daytime – and played Trivial Pursuit.

There were two teams – Sam, Rich and me versus Diane, Carl and Jem. Bec and Alex were also in attendance and Russell turned up later after Jem and Rich had left.

Of course we still partook of alcoholic refreshment but this time we had snack nibbles too and the board game gave us a new source of conversation and wisecracks.

Sam's idea is to do this once a month or so. She's suggesting that other Fridays she could stage a movie night and others still the "girls" could go out together while the "boys" stayed in. The fourth nights would be the now-traditional party in the kitchen.

Sam says this will mix it up a bit and be more interesting than just always boozing the time away. Okay, drink will still be involved but it will accompany other activities.

She asked me if Paula would be up for such an arrangement. I said I was sure that yes, work permitting, she would. I've already said that Sam and Paula like each other after one meeting, and Sam insisted on sending her a text during our game last night, which pleased me greatly.

September 29 – Happy birthday to my former work colleague and drinking buddy Lorna Lane.

It's Tuesday evening and I've just spent a wonderful two and a half days with Paula. She came over from her new home in Springbourne on Sunday afternoon and we went up to the Bell that evening.

She stayed the night with me and yesterday we went to Boscombe then hers, where we remained until this morning when she drove us back to mine and we popped back to the pub for a couple of hours this afternoon before returning here for a few hours. It's 8.30pm and she's just left.

I've thoroughly enjoyed such a long spell of quality time with the woman I love. I know she feels the same. It's been so cool just to do the normal stuff couples do together, like tour the shops, have a café meal or sit and chill listening to music.

Don't get me wrong. We do enjoy the physical side as well – and how! She makes me feel decades younger.

But it's just plain wonderful to have your best friend and your sexual partner all wrapped up in the same person. To be able to be that open and comfortable.

We don't play the silly mind games other couples do. We don't feel the need to mask, pretend, manipulate or deceive. We know each other so well, we understand each other, and accept and embrace each other's flaws and insecurities while revelling in all the positive stuff.

That's rare and very special – gold dust.

I feel so sorry for people who aren't lucky enough to have that – who can't be so frank and uninhibited with their lover so need a best pal to fulfil that vitally important supporting role.

Paula and I do that for each other. It's an equal partnership built on trust and honesty.

Oh, and we're both bonkers with the same nutty sense of humour. We laugh a lot. We have so much fun!

October 2 – Had a brilliant evening at the Bell last night – just like the good old days.

My friends Paul Dangerfield and Sarah-Jane Garbutt (previously known as Basham) have come over from Wexford, Ireland, for Paul's best mate's funeral today.

So when Paul put on Facebook that they were going to the Bell, I had to be there, even though it meant pushing my luck big time on the alcohol front this week.

It was wonderful being with that lovely couple again, and also catching up with people I hadn't seen for a while such as Roz Tidiman, Gary "Gadget" Preston and Tina McNally.

Tina's hubby Jeff, Mark "Tich" Hemington, Jem Hannen, Rich Jeffrey and John Palmer were also there and I made a new friend, Amy Wrixon, who knows many of my mates including most of the aforementioned plus Kelly Adams, Pete Rowsen and quite a few others.

Amy's also great buddies with my long-time close friend Kerry Smith. They're both avid AFC Bournemouth fans and go to many of the Cherries' matches together.

Turning to the news, nine people have been killed and seven injured in a shooting incident at a college in Oregon, America. The 26-year-old gunman opened fire at Umpqua Community College yesterday (Thursday) morning and was killed in a police shootout.

Police have not identified the attacker but officers have given the US media a name is that suggests he was born in the UK and moved to the US as a young boy.

Whoever he was, the killer's motive is not known, but the law enforcers say they were investigating reports that he had warned of his intentions on social media.

Meanwhile, the situation in the Middle East continues to deteriorate with Russia now joining in the bombing of Syria.

Several other nations, including ours, are also involved in the US-led initiative, which also extends to Afghanistan and Iraq.

The official line is that civilian casualties are being kept to a minimum and the targets are strongholds of Islamic State, a vicious and violent military organisation spreading an extreme version of the religion across the Middle East by force.

But, as usual, we can only form opinions on what we're told by untrustworthy governments and their compliant media lapdogs.

IS certainly does appear to be a very nasty piece of work – a lethally savage political movement using an intolerant form of Islam as an excuse for iron-fist control and mass bloodshed. On the face of it, it has to be forcefully resisted, just like Hitler and his Nazis.

I'm in no position to comment one way or the other. But I do say there are massive questions, not least who should be involved in halting it if that's deemed necessary.

And, of course, they should be doing it with the best of intentions, certainly not to further their own vaulting ambitions or dodgy agendas.

All the available evidence suggests that Islamic State probably is the monster it's painted as – and that it should be prevented from killing and brutalizing its opponents.

But I'm convinced that the equally brutal and arrogant imperialistic foreign policies of the US, our own governments and others operating in the Middle East over many years is at least partly to blame for the rise in IS and other fanatical radical groups.

You don't fight for peace – you peace for peace. That way you've got a far better chance of achieving it. Tit-for-tat just prolongs the agony, misery and blood-letting.

October 2, several hours later – What a lovely surprise I've had today. Phil, Emily and Chloe came over to see me and we fed nuts to the Fisherman's Walk squirrels and partook of a meal at the nearby Commodore Hotel overlooking the sea.

Well, I say fed nuts to the squirrels but in Chloe's case it was more chucking nuts in their rough direction. She also threw nuts at passing people and dogs and when we got to the pond area near the cliff top she lobbed nuts in the water to feed the fish.

My granddaughter is a real character and I adore her. Lucas and Harvey too.

The weather was warm and sunny and it was great seeing my family again and telling them all about Paula. They were really pleased for me. How cool is that?

I've asked Phil if he remembers Paula from when he was little. He's not sure. But then, he might well recognize her from Ferndown Tesco's where she's no doubt served him more than once over the years. A mate of his used to be her boss there.

I can't wait for him and Em to meet her. They're already Facebook friends.

October 5 – Happy birthday Emily, Cheryl and Joe. Hope all three have a great time.

It's Monday and I've had a pretty flipping amazing weekend.

First off there was Thursday evening's impromptu Bell reunion session with Paul, Sarah, Tina, Jeff, Roz, Gadget, Tich, Jem, Rich and others.

Then I had that lovely surprise on Friday when Phil, Emily and Chloe came to visit.

Sam invited me up to hers on Saturday afternoon for a birthday party for Rudy, who's five on Wednesday. Paula joined us later when she'd finished work and we had a great time with Sam, Carl, Diane, Bec, Alex, Tina, Jem, Russell and Kelly Adams.

Kelly's children Storm and Hudson joined Rudy and Bailey and Russell brought his two Staffie bitches Blaze and Millie, much to the delight of Albert, Becca's dog.

Paula stayed the night at my flat but had to get up early for work yesterday. She returned late morning and we sauntered through Fisherman's Walk in the warm sunshine, sitting for a while overlooking the sea before eating at the Commodore.

We returned here to chill for a few hours then last night went with Carl to the Hawkwind gig at Boscombe O2 Academy. We met Jem and Debs there.

The band were awesome, just as outstanding as the last time I saw them a couple of years ago and almost up to their standard on the classic Levitation tour back in 1980.

Paula stayed here last night but again had to get up in time to start work at Ferndown at 7am. Hope she's okay and not too tired – she's had a hectic couple of days!

October 7 – Sam and Carl, little boy Rudy is five today and Alex, Sam and Russell's son, is 21 tomorrow. Wishing them both very happy birthdays, although in Alex's case his landmark anniversary unfortunately coincides with Andy's funeral.

Well, it's nearly noon and I've had a fab 24 hours or so. Paula bussed over yesterday lunchtime and we met in the Bell for a few bevvies before getting the bus back to hers, spending the rest of the day chilling listening to music and watching one of her Ozzy Osbourne DVDs.

Paula loves her heavy rock music and is especially partial to Ozzy, Black Sabbath and Alice Cooper. She has a really cool Alice tour tee shirt from when she saw him in concert in Bournemouth in 2002.

I spent the night with her and then she drove me back home early this morning, kindly taking a detour from her journey into work at Ferndown so she could drop me off.

I didn't think it possible, but I love my woman more and more every time I see her. She feels the same and it's bloomin' marvellous!

October 9 – Today would have been John Lennon's 75th birthday had some unhinged nutter not shot him dead in New York in December 1980 when he was just 40. Happy birthday John, you inspirational legend. Listen world – war is over if you want it!

Yesterday was very sad, incredibly moving and deliciously joyous all at the same time. First off, it was Alex's 21st birthday. But just like his dad, sister, me and many others, he started it at Bournemouth Crematorium, saying goodbye to Andy Frend.

I went in a cab and arrived at the same time as Russell, Becca, Alex and Carl, who had all gone there in Russell's car. We all thought the world of Andy, a true gent if ever I knew one. A good mate, great company and very funny as well.

Also there were Jem, Fiona, Bridget and Tony Hannen, Rod Marlow, Roz Tidiman, Darren Williams, Rich and Sam Jeffrey, Jaymi Darragh, Chris and Lou Davis, Julia Pike, Sharon Pendleton, Stuart Moss, Nathan Trollope, Claire "Ping" Middleton, Gary Preston, Jem's friend Debs and many others who'd also known and loved Andy.

The service, conducted by a chaplain from the Royal Bournemouth Hospital where our buddy had passed away, was beautiful and many of us were in tears. The pain was tangible – you could feel it in the air, taste it almost.

But there was laughter too. Andy wouldn't have had it any other way. And he would have been genuinely moved and staggered by the number of family and friends turning up and the levels of affection for him on display.

Afterwards, Russell kindly gave me a lift back to Pokesdown and about an hour later most of us reconvened at the Bell for the wake, completely taking over the beer garden in the bright sunshine.

I only intended staying for a couple of pints but I couldn't tear myself away. I chatted to many people – Darren, Rod, Jem, Bridget, Debs, Roz, Jaymi, Carl, Mark "Tich" Hemington and Victoria Brown to name a few.

So much love flowed in that pub garden along with the booze and other intoxicants in people's bloodstreams. It was pretty frigging sensational – an absolutely classic session to give our mate a truly fitting send-off. That's how I want it when I go.

Lots of hugging and kissing went on as we revelled in each other's company while acutely aware that someone important was missing. Andy was one of us. But I like to think he was there in spirit, soaking up the amazing atmosphere as much as any of us.

October 11 – It's mid-morning Sunday and I've had another excellent weekend.

Friday evening Paula and I went to Sam's for a games and booze night with her, Carl, Diane and Tina. Once again Bec and Alex were also in attendance.

There was much fun and laughter as we played Trivial Pursuit again and a new game called Innuendo, where you have to answer questions against the clock with responses that can't possibly be construed to have a naughty meaning.

Trust me; it's a lot more difficult than it sounds. I very nearly said harder, which would have kinda proved the point!

Paula stayed the night with me and then went off to work early yesterday, returning at tea time after she'd finished.

We had a quiet chill-out no alcohol evening listening to music and watching DVDs and once again she stayed with me until leaving for work even earlier today.

I love spending time with my woman – sorry, can't help saying that because it sounds so good after all these years. All in all, it's been a great couple of days.

But this morning's news headlines are grim. Two explosions killed 95 people and injured hundreds when let off at a peace rally in Turkey's capital Ankara yesterday.

No group has yet claimed responsibility but the authorities are saying the suicide bombings, seconds apart, were the work of either Islamic State or Kurdish rebels.

The bombs went off just outside the capital's main train station as hundreds of opposition supporters and Kurdish activists gathered for the peace rally organized by the country's public workers' union and other groups.

The protesters had planned to demand increased democracy in Turkey and an end to renewed violence between Kurdish rebels and Turkish security forces.

Meanwhile, on a very happy note, Welsh people are celebrating after their national football team yesterday secured a place in next year's Euros alongside England. It's the first time Wales have qualified for a major tournament since 1958.

October 14 – Wishing a very happy birthday to my good friend Christine Jones, as in Tom and Chris. They're coming over some time in the next couple of weeks to shop in Bournemouth and are planning to drop in to see me on the way. Sweet!

I've had another lovely day and night with my precious Paula. She bussed over from Springbourne yesterday morning and we met in the Bell at noon as usual.

After a few lagers there we caught the bus back to her flat at tea time, stopping off at a Chinese takeaway close to hers to grab some food.

A chilled evening listening to music ensued and I stayed the night with her before she dropped me back off here early today on her way to start work at 7am.

I have a new zest for life thanks to my amazing woman. Our families and friends have commented on how happy we both appear. We're nuts about each other.

It's now noon and three hours ago I changed my Facebook status from "divorced" to "in a relationship with Paula Carruthers." It's already spurred quite a response.

But we have no plans to get wed or engaged or even live together. We've both shared homes with others and it didn't work out for either of us. We each have the tee-shirt and scars. And I did the marriage thing with Joe.

Paula and I are both quite content with the way things are. We don't live in each other's pockets and retain healthy levels of independence, emotionally, money and property-wise. We do some things together, some apart, with or without other people.

We relish our shared times and miss each other like crazy when we're not together. It keeps the whole thing fresh and interesting – exciting even – and avoids the risk of it becoming same-ish and stale and, God forbid, our taking each other for granted.

That was one of the big problems Joe and I had. We got complacent, stopped trying to keep it vibrant, started taking each other for granted and, while still talking plenty we stopped listening to each other. I don't want to make the same mistakes with Paula.

We rarely run out of things to say and even if we do it doesn't matter. Silences are comfortable when you don't feel a need to fill gaps with anything, even inane babble.

Some will see this as a lack of commitment. Not so. You don't measure that by the number of hours spent together; you define it by the depth of love and respect you have for each other and the amount of support you give emotionally and practically.

And a lot of that comes from listening to and understanding your partner.

Some people – Emily and Phil for example – see putting a ring on someone's finger as a public display of love and devotion. For them it's a pure, heart-warming impulse.

But others use engagement and wedding bands as a control mechanism. Their message is clear: "You're mine and this will stop you even looking at others, let alone straying to explore pastures new."

This is mad. If someone's going to cheat, they'll do it anyway and trying to stop them with a piece of metal or paper – children even – won't make a blind bit of difference.

Quite the reverse, in fact – getting too paranoid and possessive will simply drive them into someone else's arms sooner rather than later.

And, at the end of the day, surely this is the crux of the matter? You can't possibly love someone without trusting them implicitly. If you don't, something's very wrong.

Paula and I speak candidly about such things and I'm a great believer in being honest from the outset because nurturing false hopes and dreams can be ultimately extremely corrosive, leading to resentment and bitterness.

But having said all that, if the last three months or so has proved anything to us two it's that plans can alter as fate intervenes to completely overhaul views and overturn circumstances, transforming lives in the most dramatic of ways.

So I guess what I'm saying is this is the situation as we both currently see it and neither of us can perceive that changing in the foreseeable future. But who knows?

As always, I think it's a case of watch this space.

Turning to more mundane matters, England have qualified for the Euros in France next year with a 100 per cent record, winning all 10 of their matches in the group stage. They achieved it with a 3-0 win over Lithuania.

And Northern Ireland went through top of their group, securing their place alongside England and Wales. Sadly, Scotland missed out again.

October 15 – Flippin' 'eck! Yesterday's Facebook status changing my details from "divorced" to "in a relationship" has drawn my biggest reaction ever – 45 "likes" and over a dozen comments. It's wonderful that family and mates are pleased for us.

But now methinks it's time for a little more metaphysical meandering.

The rise in tension and bloodshed across the world is the end result of violent clashes stemming from deeply damaging cultural and ethnic differences. Ironically, religion – or rather mankind's warped interpretations of it – appears to be at the heart of all this.

Christianity, Judaism, Islam, whatever – followers of dogmatic, rigid faiths often get it so wrong, such is the critical amount of brainwashing they receive from dark masters whose brutal and wicked agendas have nothing to do with spirituality or enlightenment.

Sin and punishment, guilt and retribution, repentance and salvation – control, control, control. We need to open our minds and free our souls, sisters and brothers. It's the only possible way we can even begin to grasp the truth.

Or have I just had too much tea over the years?

****

CHAPTER NINE
GOOD TIMES, UNLUCKY CLASHES

October 19 – Wishing a very happy birthday to Sam Lowney, bar manageress at the Bell. She loves animals, especially dogs, and is very nice lady.

It's Monday and I've had an excellent weekend. Friday evening Paula and I went to Sam's for another boozy board games evening with her, Carl, Tina, Jem and Rich – the first time she'd met him. The boys, Bec, Albert and the cats were also there.

Paula stayed the night at mine and went off to work rather hung over Saturday morning. I felt rough too. We had a chill out evening in our own homes and she returned here yesterday lunch time after doing three hours' overtime in the morning.

Phil and Emily also came over, bringing Chloe and Lucas. We all went for a saunter through Fisherman's Walk before having a meal at the Commodore Hotel.

It was great that my son and his wife met Paula for the first time and even better that they got on so well. The children really took to her too, especially Lucas. Cool!

Yesterday evening Paula and I went up to the Bell where we met and chatted to our mutual pal John Gaynor. She stayed the night and went off to work from here first thing this morning.

As I said, it was an excellent weekend. And Paula's coming back here after work this evening to stay the night as we're not doing our usual Tuesday meet-up tomorrow – she's catching up with a female friend.

October 26 – I've had another marvellous weekend with my amazing woman. The reason behind this was irksome, inconvenient and ultimately deeply frustrating. But it was still lovely to spend three days with her.

She came to mine Friday, stayed the night and Saturday lunchtime we moved on to her flat and based ourselves there until early this (Monday) morning when again she dropped me off at home on her way to work.

It gave me a chance to check out Paula's local pub. Very nice it was too. Called the Cricketers Arms, it's a five minute walk from hers. Small, cosy with nice people.

I'm back off to Paula's on the bus tomorrow to spend another day and night with her – it's a Tuesday, her usual day off work. I'm feeling pretty privileged at the moment I can tell you.

As well as the rather irksome reason behind it, our weekend together unfortunately coincided with three lovely offers for us to join other people, which we couldn't do.

First off, Tom text me early last week saying that he and Chris were coming to Bournemouth on Friday to do some shopping, have a few drinks in a town centre pub in the evening and stay the night in a hotel. Did I want to join them?

Under normal circumstances I would have been well up for it, and I told him so. It was just the worst possible timing, that's all. Never mind, maybe next time.

Saturday Sam text Paula to ask if we wanted to pop up to hers that evening for a few bevvies. Again, we had to decline.

Then yesterday (Sunday) morning. Phil sent Paula a private Facebook message asking if we wanted to go to his and Emily's at Ferndown to spend some time with them and watch the new *Jurassic World* movie.

He'd also sent me a similar Facebook message but of course I was away from my computer for a couple of days so I didn't see it until this morning (he and Paula have the social site on their phones and Paula also has it on her electronic tablet).

It was a very sweet gesture and showed me just how much he and Em like Paula, which I'd kinda gathered already but it was nice to have it confirmed that way.

Again, as with Tom and Chris, hopefully we can do it some other time soon.

But, all the clashes and hassles aside, it was still another great weekend with the woman I love to bits.

I've just read some very sad news on Facebook. Celtic Nicky, an amiable feller and Bell stalwart for many years, has passed on. I've referred to him briefly in my books.

I'll never forget how he used to get hold of discount Manchester United stuff and sell it to me for a bargain price so I could give it to Phil when he was a boy and I used to take him to the pub on Sunday afternoons.

More recently, Paula and I have seen Nicky there regularly on our visits to the Bell on Tuesday afternoons. RIP friend – till we meet again.

October 28 – Sometimes we all need to say sorry for the things we've said and done. But no-one should ever apologize for being who they are, the views they hold or the way they lead their life – as long as they don't cause too much pain and hurt to others along the way.

We should all try constantly to be better people, but those who can't accept and respect us for us – inconsistencies, insecurities, irrational fears, irritating traits, warts, flaws and all – should keep the hell away.

October 31 – Happy Halloween folks! Yep, it's that time of year again for scary costumes, blood-curdling movies and trick or treating.

Or, on a more serious note, a sacred and important night for followers of the nature religions – a key turning point of the year when the veil between conventional reality and the spirit world is said to be at its thinnest.

And on a much more serious note, real-life horror stories continue to fill the news.

A Russian airliner carrying more than 200 people has crashed in central Sinai, Egypt.

The Airbus A-321 had just left the Red Sea resort of Sharm el-Sheikh, bound for St Petersburg.

Wreckage of the plane has been found in the Hassana area. It disappeared from radar screens when travelling at 9,500m (31,000ft), Egyptian officials said.

Meanwhile, 27 people have died and 155 been injured after fire broke out at a night club in Bucharest, Romania. The blaze is believed to have been caused by fireworks let off inside the building.

Terrible tidings indeed, but there is also far happier news a lot closer to home.

Today is my friend Jane Marshall's birthday. She's a lovely person with a sweet temperament and compassionate views who smiles a lot. I know her from when she used to do the weekly quiz at the Bell with her brother. Happy birthday Jane.

November 3 – Halloween turned out to be a bit of a nightmare in the end.

Paula and I went to Sam's for her usual themed fancy dress party. The event itself, on Saturday 31st, was largely fine – the customary fun session in fact – but there were one or two niggles this time around that took the shine off it.

The real drama came afterwards. Paula losing her expensive mobile phone was the main hassle in a catalogue of minor disasters causing upset and heated exchanges.

She replaced it with another costly one the next day – Sunday – but she was understandably a very angry, unhappy bunny. A ferocious hangover didn't help.

All in all, the last two weekends have been a pretty testing time for our relationship, for different reasons. But we're solid. We love each other to pieces and are equally determined to take the rough with the smooth.

Meanwhile, in the news, an external influence is thought to be responsible for the weekend's plane crash tragedy in Egypt.

The Russian Airbus 321 is believed to have broken up in mid-air over the Sinai Peninsula on Saturday, killing all 224 people on board.

Was it a terrorist attack – and if so, by whom? Speculation is rife as site investigations continue.

November 3, 6pm – Paula was with a female pal today so we didn't do our usual Tuesday meet up. I went to the Bell alone to honour Celtic Nicky at the wake following his funeral. The place was packed, showing how highly he was regarded.

Nicky was a Bell legend, a total gentleman. Farewell pal, see you on the other side.

November 6 – Yesterday provided a very pleasant break from the norm for this slavish creature of routine. And no, it had nothing to do with Bonfire Night.

Paula came over early evening after finishing work and having her hair cut and she spent the rest of the day and the night with me, leaving here to drive to work early this morning.

It was the first time she'd come over on a Thursday, but then we were missing each other so terribly and we had to make up for Tuesday when we didn't link up as usual.

I know I've mentioned this before but I just can't stop saying it – I love that woman so much and I love spending time with her, especially in her arms. It's blooming ace!

November 7 – They say sarcasm is the lowest form of wit. But it's such good fun!

November 11, 11.20 am – It's Armistice Day and I've just observed the two minutes' silence along with millions of other people across the UK.

Unfortunately an ignorant idiot neighbour with no respect for our war dead insisted on using a power tool in his garden throughout most of it. Shame on him!

It's always a sombre occasion, marking the end of the First World War and remembering all those brave service folk in conflicts from then till now who have been cruelly sacrificed on the blood drenched altar of political lunacy.

Like most folk, I do so both on Armistice Day itself and Remembrance Sunday, when we watch the obscene and sickening spectacle of the politicians who get us into the wars laying poppy wreaths at the Cenotaph in London.

But to turn to much nicer matters, yesterday was a joyous one for your loopy narrator.

Paula and I went to Ali and Terry's wedding at Poole Guildhall and then to afternoon tea – or in our case, a couple of pints of lager – to help celebrate their happy union.

Paula loved seeing Phil, Emily and Chloe again and it was the first time she'd met Harvey, Ali, Terry, their two little daughters, Joe, Stuart, Gail, Rachel and little Lily.

It was also the first time I'd met Isabella, Ali and Terry's baby girl. I've seen Roxanna, their adorable toddler, several times at family dos.

And, small world innit? – Paula discovered she knew one of Ali's bridesmaids, so had a chat with her and her feller and exchanged phone numbers with them.

But that wasn't the end of our celebrations. Later in the day, Paula got a phone call from her son's partner Emma telling her she was a grandma again. Emma and Matt, Paula's son, had just been blessed with a baby girl Mattea.

They already have one young daughter, Georjeana, who's the spitting image of Paula when she was the same age.

I felt so privileged to be with Paula when she received her happy tidings and share in that extra special moment. That's what relationships are all about, isn't it? – relishing the great times while facing and confronting the not so good ones together and united?

November 13 – More sad news on the music front… Phil "Philthy Animal" Taylor has died at the age of just 61.

He's probably best known as a former drummer with heavy rockers Motorhead. Those of you who have read my book *Scratched Crystal* will know that I met him, very briefly, when I had my life-changing encounter with band front man Lemmy backstage at the group's Poole Arts Centre gig in October 1978.

Still with music, this week ITV broadcast a two-hour show featuring the nation's favourite Beatles number ones as chosen by viewers.

The top four were all Paul McCartney compositions – 1, Hey Jude: 2, Yesterday; 3, Let It Be and 4, Eleanor Rigby, with Lennon's All You Need is Love at number five.

George Harrison's classic Something, the only song written by him to be contemporaneously released as a Beatles single, also made the list.

But before any bright spark points out, quite rightly, that Something and Let It Be weren't actually UK number ones and Yesterday only hit number eight when released as a single here six years after the group broke up, the poll included not only their 17 UK chart-toppers but also the other 10 that reached number one in the United States.

So it included the Long and Winding Road and Eight Days a Week, not released as singles here, and Love Me Do, which only reached number 17 in Britain when put out as their debut single but later clinched the top spot in America after the band had taken that country by storm.

It got to number four here when re-released in 1982 to mark its 20th anniversary.

Oh, and contrary to what many think, including even some Beatles fans, Please Please Me only got to number two in the nation's official BBC listings although topping other UK charts, and Free as a Bird and Penny Lane also stalled at the runner-up slot.

Obviously I thoroughly enjoyed the programme and as it got to its climax with Hey Jude, my mind slipped back immediately to my times at the Reading Rock Festival in the 1970s and the much-missed legendary deejay John Peel.

For those who don't know, Peel was a pioneer who gave many future rock stars their first big breaks on Radio One – whether they had recording contracts or not.

While others played it safe following the rather conservative BBC company line, he went out on a limb time and time again, showing impeccable taste in the process.

From T Rex, Hawkwind, David Bowie, Genesis and Mike Oldfield to the Ramones, the Undertones, Talking Heads and the Fall, he played the stuff no-one else on mainstream radio would dare to – and won so much respect from music fans keen to hear fresh and exciting new sounds.

Back in the mid-seventies Peel would always fill the deejay spot on Saturday evenings at Reading, the last set before the headline act on the festival's biggest night. And he'd always play two songs guaranteed to get the crowd in the mood.

One was Freebird by Lynyrd Skynyrd. The other was Hey Jude.

And he had a charming little chant he encouraged his audience of tens of thousands to shout at top volume, saying he really wanted to piss of the neighbours.

It went: "John Peel's a c*nt!" Peely, we love you man. What a legend!

November 14 – There's very bad news indeed from across the Channel. More than 125 people were killed and 200 injured as bombers and gunmen ran riot in Paris last (Friday) night.

There were eight separate terrorist attacks across the city in the worst violent atrocity to hit France since World War Two. Islamic extremists have been blamed, a state of emergency declared and three days of mourning announced.

Shock, trauma, sadness, bitterness and anger are rife in our battered neighbour country as Britain and other European nations step up security measures and show solidarity with the French.

American president Barack Obama has also condemned the horrific savagery of the attacks. It's believed all the terrorists died.

While France comes to terms with last night's events, here in Pokesdown we're meeting at the Bell today for a charity fundraiser in memory of our mate Andy Frend.

The money will go to his two children and the Macmillan cancer care fund.

Andy's close pal Rich Jeffery is sacrificing his beloved long hair and beard to help encourage people to donate. This is a huge deal for Rich and he has our respect.

I saw him last night as Sam and Carl staged another hilarious board game and booze evening. Tina Mcauley, Jem Hannen and Sam's cousin Diane were also there.

Paula couldn't make it this time as she was on a late finish at Ferndown Tesco's yesterday with an early start this morning. But I will see her later today when she comes over after work for the Bell money spinner and to stay the night at mine.

Needless to say, I've missed her like mad since I said goodbye to her early Wednesday morning after spending Tuesday night at her place.

November 15 – Yesterday's Bell charity shindig was brilliant with loads of friends coming together to support the cause – far too many to mention here. And yes, Rich is now bald as a coot and clean shaven. Nice one buddy!

November 16, 11.15am – Like millions of people across the world, I've just observed a minute's silence for the 129 victims now known to have died as a result of Friday's terrorist attacks on Paris.

The grisly toll is expected to rise even further for there are still scores of people critically ill in hospital.

Meanwhile, political leaders are talking tough, threatening to hit back hard after this "act of war." Oh dear – when will it ever cease? When oh when will negotiations, compromise and peace replace hostility, bloody-mindedness and violence?

I fear not in my lifetime. And that depresses the hell out of me, I can tell you.

Turning to much lighter matters, I'm delighted that the new series of *I'm a Celebrity Get Me out of Here* started yesterday evening on ITV.

Telly presenter Yvette Fielding, former footballer Kieron Dyer, Spandau Ballet singer Tony Hadley and boxing legend Chris Eubank are among this year's participants. Plus a charmingly eccentric aristocrat called Lady Colin Campbell who looks like she'll provide some top-notch entertainment.

Speaking of celebrities, we had the sad news over the weekend of the passing of Warren Mitchell, the man who immortalized legendary comedy character Alf Garnett.

Mitchell, 89, had apparently been ill for a while but was said to be cracking jokes right to the end.

A versatile actor who could perform serious material as well as make us chuckle, he will always be associated with working class Tory bigot Alf, one of the greatest sitcom figures ever created for British television.

Although poles apart from Alf in political terms, I grew up loving him in Johnny Speight's classic show *Till Death Us Do Part*, where the brilliant Mitchell was very ably supported by Dandy Nicholls, Una Stubbs and Tony Booth – Cherie Blair's dad.

And Mitchell himself had very different views to Alf. A left-wing, Jewish Tottenham Hotspurs fan, he was greatly amused by the irony of playing a Conservative-voting, Royalist, pseudo-Christian West Ham supporter.

But he was worried that some right-wing nuts took Alf seriously, praising his outspoken rants against foreigners, gays and socialists and totally failing to see that Till Death was satire and Speight and he were actually parodying such views.

Farewell Alf – RIP and thanks for all the laughs.

November 18 – Yesterday, a Tuesday, was lovely. Paula came over and we went to the Bell for a few pints before leaving tea-time to pick up fish and chips on the way back to my flat, where we chilled for the evening then retired early for the night.

It's always great to spend time in the company – and then the arms – of the gorgeous lady who's made me happier than I thought I could possibly be ever again.

Paula got up in the dark at stupid o'clock this morning to get to work for an early start. Several hours later, I caught the bus to the

Royal Bournemouth Hospital to keep my annual heart check appointment with my cardiac consultant Dr Rozkovec.

The monitoring machine showed that my replacement valve was still leaking blood and still deteriorating, but not to the extent to cause him undue concern. So once again it was "look after yourself, see you same time next year." Phew, that's a relief!

Next door to the hospital is the hotel where Ferndown Tesco's are holding their staff Christmas party in two and a bit weeks' time. Passing it on the bus coming home, I thought of what I might say if any of Paula's workmates ask me that rather pointless, tiresome, dumb, unimaginative and irritating question: "What do you do for a living?"

Rather than yawn, I'll probably respond with something like: "I'm a writer. I was a journalist but retired early through ill health and now I'm a published author."

Which might well inspire a follow-up question along the lines of: "What sort of books do you write – fiction or non-fiction?"

Then I thought of how to explain the content of my ongoing journal in amusing terms without getting bogged down in tedious, unnecessary and ultimately boring details.

My reply could thus be: "I'm a diarist and lyric writer – A sort of cross between Bridget Jones, Samuel Pepys and Tim Rice." Yep, that'll do if I'm asked – by Paula's colleagues at that event or anyone else from now on for that matter.

November 20 – It's a week on from that terrible killing spree in Paris and the deep trauma has turned to bitter anger and a demand that violent Islamic extremists are violently wiped out.

Oh great! – All that does is fan the flames of hostility and hatred and make matters far worse. Fighting fire with fire never solves problems and just perpetuates the misery with more people suffering and dying.

It's a pity the politicians don't follow Conservative Prime Minister John Major's example when dealing with the IRA back in the 1990s after they'd started bombing mainland UK targets as the tension over Northern Ireland reached fever pitch.

Basically, he told them: "Right, you have my attention – let's talk."

And it was that attitude – so refreshing after Thatcher's confrontational and insane declaration that "we don't negotiate with terrorists" – that paved the way for what became the historic Good Friday agreement that at last put the province on the road to peace after decades of war and bloodshed.

Yes, the initiative was Major's, not Labour PM Tony Blair's – he just happened to be in power when the agreement was finally signed. And his later warlike policies over Afghanistan and Iraq showed us what he really was – a ruthless aggressor.

He's still stoking the fires of hatred now with his brutally insensitive calls for even more intensely violent military involvement in the Middle East, and especially Syria.

Others are making similar demands. The official line is that the murderous nut jobs of Islamic State are using those lands – and Syria in particular – as safe havens while carrying out their bombing, shooting and killing campaigns across the world.

Millions of people in France, England, Germany and other European countries, America, Australia, Canada and territories elsewhere are now backing the politicians' hard line stances and actions.

Meanwhile, peace-loving Muslims fear for their lives as a savage backlash seems inevitable and we brace ourselves for a new global war. It's all so very depressing.

But this observer firmly believes that arrogant and aggressive meddling in the Middle East by our own political leaders and those of France, America and other nations since the Second World War has been a major reason for the widespread suspicion and hatred of the West that's led directly the rise of IS and other extremist groups.

And, just like with any other war or revolution, I fear a savage, self-serving network of despicable individuals is callously funding both sides, not caring how many people get hurt just so long as they maintain control while amassing more money and power.

Where does IS get its cash and other resources? Now that, my friends, is a very good question indeed. Do you think we're gonna get a straight answer? – Nah, me neither.

And let's face it; Syria was in the meddlers' sights all along. All they needed was the public backing for their cold and brutal ambitions. Now it seems they've got it – and those poor French people were sacrificed to make sure they did. It sickens me greatly.

Just to clarify, I'm no apologist for terrorism or any acts of violence resulting in death and pain. I hate such behaviour with a passion, no matter who's responsible.

I just firmly believe that we're being spoon fed an official version of current events that's far too black and white, goodies and baddies, suiting certain unscrupulous manipulators right down to the ground.

As always, the reality is far more complex, subtle and puzzling and the actual facts very hard to find, they're so well hidden. If we knew them, we'd be staggered.

Conspiracy theorists speak of a scenario they call "problem reaction solution." You have a plan but you know people won't support it because it's too extreme. So you create a situation, a crisis leading to widespread calls for something to be done.

At that point, you come forward with your original intention, proposing it as the answer in the confident belief that now it will be accepted as such. Bingo!

Is there any truth in this or is it just crazy talk, wild speculation? As events unfold I'm becoming increasingly convinced – and that scares the crap out of me, I can tell you.

Others will pooh-pooh any such notion, and I respect their right to do so. Am I losing the plot, or are they in firm denial because they're bloody terrified to even accept the possibility because it would shake their worldview to its foundations? Who knows?

November 21 (Saturday) – Continuing the theme of the truth being deliberately concealed from us, this does beg the obvious question – how the hell can anyone make informed decisions when not in possession of all the available facts?

It's a crucial query covering all eventualities from personal relationships to global situations. Lies and deception, smoke and mirrors, blah de blah de blah! Yeah right!

November 21 – several hours later... I've just had a quite stupendous day which was totally unexpected. Phil contacted me this morning asking if I had any plans for my Saturday and if not could he and Emily come over?

I replied of course they could, and it took off from there. They arrived with my adorable granddaughter Chloe and we had coffee and a catch-up at mine before Phil drove us to a West Moors restaurant, the Tap and Railway, where we had a meal.

Just before arriving, we passed the Elephant and Castle – the pub across the road from where Paula lived until moving to Springbourne in September.

After that, we went to Phil and Em's place, where we chilled watching movies until they dropped me off back here at my flat.

It was quite wonderful spending time with the family and especially Chloe, who's getting to the age where she can hold conversations and didn't leave me alone. Cool!

I thoroughly enjoyed the experience but had two regrets. One was that Lucas and Harvey weren't there. The other was that my Paula wasn't either – she was at work.

November 22 – Happy 26th birthday Phil… My son, pride and joy, constant source of sanity and inspiration and main reason to live for the past quarter-century or so.

****

CHAPTER TEN – THE DEMON DRINK

November 23 – Icy weather has finally hit the UK after one of the longest, warmest autumns on record.

Okay, granted, winter doesn't officially start until the solstice on December 21, but you try telling that to people suddenly shivering in the cold.

Elsewhere in the world, at least 22 are known to have been killed in a terrorist attack on a Mali hotel.

Gunmen thought to be Islamic militants are said to have burst in and opened fire on guests gathering for breakfast.

And in New Zealand, four Brits, two Australians and the local pilot have died in a helicopter crash.

My own weekend has been much nicer. After Saturday's pleasant surprise of spending time with Phil, Emily and Chloe, I had another fine day yesterday (Sunday) when Paula came over at noon to be with me for the rest of the day and night.

We had a meal and a few pints at the Commodore before chilling for the evening listening to Pink Floyd albums at mine.

While at the pub, one of the many things we chatted about was the effect booze has on people.

It's often said that we speak the truth when drunk. But that's not quite right. As usual, it's more complicated than that – and ultimately more risky and troublesome.

Alcohol consumption certainly removes inhibitions and loosens up our minds and our tongues. But a dulling of the perception and senses means there's frequently a huge difference between what we mean to say and what actually comes out of our mouths.

I've messed up many times, unintentionally upsetting someone by clumsily phrasing my words. This gets especially frustrating when something intended as a compliment ends up sounding like a criticism. I find it's alarmingly easily done.

There may be a louder ring of truth in what we utter under the influence, but it can emerge as a twisted and far darker version of what we're actually trying to say.

And that's what causes emotional injury, friction and arguments. I guess that's one reason it's called the demon drink.

It can get especially messy when you throw technological gadgets into the equation. Trying to use Facebook or a mobile phone when tipsy or worse can have very dire consequences indeed.

People say the daftest things when they're drunk. And, of course, a text or Facebook declaration appears in cold, hard letters without the subtleties of the spoken word.

This can be a problem even when you're stone cold sober, because as you read someone's comments in stark black and white you're not getting those vital voice inflections that tell you if they're joking or being serious.

So much misunderstanding and unnecessary hurt can be caused – and it's ten times worse if people have been drinking.

Having said all that, I have trouble with machines, tools and other and devices anyway. I'm the least practical man in the world. Technology and me just don't mix – I still struggle with the concept of pencils!

November 24 – Wishing a very happy birthday to my sister, Carol. I put some money in a card and posted it off to Selsey the other day. She and David are coming over in a couple of weeks' time for our annual pre-Christmas present exchange and meal out with Suzette.

This time Paula's going to join us as she has that day off work. It will be nice for her to meet more of my family.

November 29 – The world turned a shade darker 14 years ago today… George Harrison passed away. I've lit a candle for him and I'm playing one of his albums as I type this. I put a little tribute to him on Facebook a bit earlier.

Apart from missing the musical maestro and his profound wisdom, my second thought today was along the lines of strewth! – Where the heck did those 14 years go?

Actually that's not quite right – in truth these were my second and third thoughts this morning. The first was how badly I was missing Paula, absent from my flat after spending the previous two nights here. I'll see her again on Tuesday.

Friday (27th) was also a sad day for music fans – it would have marked Jimi Hendrix's 73rd birthday had he not died in 1970 aged 27. He was another guitar playing genius.

It was a good day for me though. Paula had time off work so came over Thursday evening, staying until early Saturday apart from a brief excursion back to her place Friday morning. The afternoon was spent in the Bell and the evening chilling at mine.

In the outside world, David Cameron is poised to once again ask the Commons to back air strikes on Syria in response to Paris and other recent terrorist attacks.

Labour leader Jeremy Corbyn is against such aggression, saying he would prefer a peaceful resolution to problems in the Middle East and is far from convinced that all other options have yet been exhausted. I think he's right.

Warmongering Tories are predictably banging on about defending our country and putting immense pressure on their Labour counterparts to support Cameron's plan.

I greatly fear the hawks will win the day – again – and Corbyn, a breath of fresh air in modern-day politics as far as I'm concerned, could well be a casualty in the mad rush to engage in further military intervention in the Middle East with no thought of the likely disastrous repercussions for the Syrians and us alike.

ISIS is a nettle that has to be grasped. But, like Corbyn, I'm deeply concerned, feeling that plunging into war and shutting off communication channels isn't the answer.

Some crazed MPs are even talking wildly about wiping ISIS off the face of the Earth. Like that will ever happen you ridiculous morons! – They'll just come back stronger and more bitterly aggrieved than ever.

No, the only sensible, logical solution is to use diplomacy, negotiation and compromise in an attempt to find the way forward to a more peaceful future.

But there I go again, being hopelessly naïve. While millions of us on all sides are desperate to live in harmony, there's always a belligerent minority wanting division and extreme violence. The problem is that many of them are in positions of power.

They're the ones who cause the wars. But they never get their own hands dirty. That's left to decent, trusting patriots who put their lives on the line in battle zones.

They're the ones who suffer and die. They're the ones who come back physically and mentally devastated and end up sleeping in doorways because the politicians don't give a monkey's about them. You've served your purpose, now you're on your own!

And peace-loving civilians, whether Parisian, Syrian, Londoners or New Yorkers, are being sacrificed en masse on the bloodstained altar of political, ideological insanity.

Or is it just the vaulting, twisted ambition of cold-hearted, selfish, greedy individuals operating in networks and ruthlessly using different worldviews to their own ends?

I'm far from convinced that Islamic extremists are behind all the atrocities being blamed on them. Some, yes probably, but all? – I suspect not. Methinks someone's very busy stirring up friction and resentment between ethnic groups.

It's a crying shame no-one with influence is using as much energy addressing the problems at root, asking the obvious but incredibly inconvenient question (for some) – what causes the extreme bitterness and anger that spurs people to kill and maim?

No-one in their right mind wants the bloodshed and misery to continue. Surely we all just want to live in peace and be left alone to pursue our own religious and cultural lifestyles unmolested – while respecting others' right to do the same? Am I wrong?

If I am, I really do despair!

November 30 – Well done lionesses! Our England ladies football team beat Bosnia 1-0 yesterday (Sunday) in their qualifying match for the Euros. Meanwhile, the Scottish women thrashed Macedonia 10-0.

And speaking of Scots, Andy Murray and brother Jamie were in the tennis playing team that won the Davis Cup for Great Britain yesterday for the first time since 1936.

And in my little corner of the world, I'm delighted for Paula, who starts a well-earned week off work today.

She found a great quote on the internet yesterday that she borrowed and put on Facebook as a status. It was along the lines of:

"Be with someone who accepts your craziness and still loves you rather than an idiot who tries to make you normal."

I really like that, because it applies to us, or more precisely, her attitude to me. It's brilliant that she accepts and embraces me as I am, flaws and infuriating quirks and all, and still loves me without trying to change me.

And you know what? The beautiful irony is that as a result she IS actually changing me, thanks to how she makes me feel and the confidence boost she's given me.

Sitting watching TV last night, a new lyric formed in my head. It was about how time whizzes past you faster as you get older. Here it is:

THE BLINK OF AN EYE

Martin Money, November 29–30, 2015

I fear my life has passed me by – gone in the blink of an eye

It seems like only yesterday I sat on splintered chairs
As teachers wrote in chalk on slate and sang of woods and bears

It doesn't feel that long ago my passion blazed so strong
My dreams were still intact and how my soul yearned to belong

I fear my life has passed me by – gone in the blink of an eye

Why did the years speed by so fast to leave me high and dry?
I gaze and wonder what went wrong under this leaden sky

It's quite amazing to think back to times with golden rings
So long ago but now I have the joy a grandchild brings

And now I have the love of a great woman I adore
It's just a shame we didn't take our chance for this before

I fear my life has passed me by – gone in the blink of an eye.

November 30, several hours later – Ey up! Another one has also formed, sparked by the approach of the festive season:

PANTOMIME

Martin Money, November 29–30, 2015

It's time to share a Christmas song and plead for peace on Earth
To talk of love, goodwill to all and smile for what it's worth
So put those decorations up, dust off your festive trees
As politicians wage their wars against old enemies

As winter showers drizzle down and freeze me to my bones
Those icy winds remind me of the chill of battle zones
Coz coldness is a way of life and fighting kills off dreams
Between the ones in uniforms and all of us it seems

It's all just a pantomime with villains by the score
Their masks and costumes cannot hide the evil I abhor

The snow and Santa scenes that fill our homes and
   shopping streets
Are light years from reality that false ideal deletes
Or tries to but will never truly manage to succeed
So long as people have the will to cut till others bleed

As money rules our way of life in savage tinsel town
The ad men hit the overdrive to stop us getting down
But party time means alcohol which makes us all lash out
And no-one gives a thought to what it's meant to be about

It's all just a pantomime with villains by the score
Their masks and costumes cannot hide the evil I abhor.

And, just for good measure, I'll chuck in another philosophical thought:

In any sphere of life, when the bad times outweigh the good, you should make your exit and find pastures new.

December 3 – I've just got back from two super days with Paula during which we based ourselves at her Springbourne flat.

We went shopping in Winton, had a few pints in the Cricketers and started off in Boscombe, where she had another Black Sabbath tattoo – this time on the other arm – done at Scribe and we had a couple of drinks in the Bell, across the road opposite.

It was terrific spending so much time with my lady, who I'm seeing again tomorrow and also Saturday, when we go to the Tesco's staff Christmas party.

She finishes her week off and returns to work on Monday.

On the global stage, we're at war again because the Commons voted by 397 to 223 to send in the bomber planes to hit ISIS bases in Syria.

This has been so depressingly predictable for at least two years now and it's bad news indeed. I fear an escalation of the violence with more terrorist attacks on civilians and another major conflict comparable to the two world wars. Merry Christmas!

December 6 – I've just had another great couple of days with Paula. Friday we had a few drinks in the Bell and I was delighted to be reunited with my friends Al and Debs, two former regulars at the pub.

Last night (Saturday) I accompanied Paula to the Ferndown Tescos staff Christmas party in a hotel called the Village, across the road from the Royal Bournemouth Hospital.

It was a super shindig and I met and talked to several really smashing people. I can see why Paula loves working alongside them and doesn't want to move to a branch nearer her new home.

She finishes her week's holiday today and returns to work tomorrow – but has Tuesday off as usual so I'll see her again then.

On a more serious note, the worsening crisis in the Middle East and our involvement in yet another war there really makes me fear for the futures of my grandchildren.

What sort of messed up, violent and unstable world are we creating for them?

December 7 – Vicky Pattison is the new queen of the jungle. The gutsy, funny and endearing 28-year-old was crowned last night after winning the latest series of *I'm a Celebrity Get Me Out Of Here*.

I must confess I'd never heard of her before but apparently she made her name on another reality TV show called *Geordie Shore*, based in her native Newcastle.

George Shelley, 21, of the boy band Union J was runner up and another girl who made her name on reality TV, Ferne McCann, 25, came third.

Ferne's claim to fame is being in the popular programme *The Only Way is Essex.*

I hadn't heard of any of them before their jungle adventures – not being a big fan of either boy bands or reality shows, except Celebrity of course, which I love.

But the three plucky and charming youngsters beat their older and more established campmates such as Tony Hadley, Yvette Fielding, Kieron Dyer and Chris Eubank as they won over the viewing public that voted to keep them in the contest.

The big shock for me was the fact that Lady Colin Campbell, or Lady C as she became known, turned from a quirky and entertaining aristocrat into a venom-spitting monster before our eyes.

She ended up being the most arrogant, obnoxious and controversial participant in the show's 15-year history – but she made for some compelling television all the same.

You know you're approaching Christmas when this fascinating TV show reaches its climax. It's one of the highlights of my TV viewing year.

And this year's three young finalists were all in their twenties, as is my own son, Phil, who's recently turned 26.

His older brother John, who was stillborn, would have been 27 today. I've lit a candle for him. Forever loved, never forgotten. You learn to deal with such things but the deep scars never heal and stay with you for life.

Changing the subject completely, Paula's home patch of Cumbria has been among the worst hit areas after weekend storms brought severe flooding to some parts of the UK.

TV news pictures over the past couple of days have shown Carlisle and other nearby places under several feet after torrential rain poured down and rivers burst their banks.

December 9 – Oh dear! Carol and David were supposed to be coming over yesterday for our annual pre-Christmas meal, catch-up and cards and presents exchange but had to cancel because David had been taken ill during the previous night, wasn't well enough to drive and they'd arranged for him to see his doctor later that day.

This was a massive shame because it meant I didn't see Suzette either and none of them got the chance to meet Paula, who was accompanying me this time around.

I was so looking forward to introducing more of my family to my amazing lady.

As mentioned in previous books, the normal routine is for David and Carol to pick me up in their car and then drive to Suzette's Parkstone home to collect her as well on the way to the Toby Carvery at Fleetsbridge Roundabout just outside Poole.

I dearly hope David's okay and it wasn't anything too serious. I wish him a speedy recovery.

Carol's cancellation meant I spent the day – a Tuesday – with just Paula. We went to the Bell for a few drinks, got the bus back to hers, had a kebab take-away each then popped into the Cricketers for a couple, returning to hers to spend the night together.

As usual, she dropped me back off at my place early this morning on the way to work.

Yesterday was also the sad anniversary of John Lennon's murder on December 8, 1980. I put a tribute to him on Facebook – a song lyric I wrote just after his shocking death. John's calls for peace and an end to all war are more poignant and relevant than ever in these dark, violent and uncertain times.

Oh, and *Sunshine and Ice Volume Seven: Persistent Illusions* has been out a year today.

December 11 – Isn't it interesting when people are quite happy to dish it out but can't take it in return?

This applies in many of life's differing scenarios, from sarcasm and insults to outright violence. But I'm thinking here especially of speaking about others to third parties when they're not present.

Some folk seem to relish in constantly bad mouthing their loved ones and friends to others but are severely put out when they think the same thing's happening to them.

These people often resort to spreading malicious gossip, badly twisting the truth or even telling lies. But they're paranoid when they even suspect they're getting it back.

Let's face it, we all talk about our mates, colleagues and loved ones to others when they're not around. It would be stupidly naïve to think that we don't. It's a perfectly natural and normal impulse because these people are part of our lives.

But it crosses the line when it gets nasty and hurtful – especially if what's being said is gross exaggeration, an incorrect reflection of the facts or, even worse, untrue.

This is particularly commonplace when conversations and comments are reported to a third party with the innocent or intended addition of a potentially damaging spin.

I know my friends and loved ones speak about me behind my back. Of course they do. I talk about them to others too. It would be very strange if this wasn't the case.

But I aim to keep my facts straight and I try to give accurate accounts. I refuse to spread untruths or sinisterly twisted gossip. I would never do that. A bit of harmless gossip maybe, but that's all.

And if I do get it slightly wrong in relaying it to another person, it's always an innocent mistake, never a deliberate perversion or blatant lie.

Of course, we all occasionally feel the need to offload our frustrations with our nearest and dearest to a neutral, impartial person outside that particular relationship – whatever it is, a partnership, close friendship or other significant human interaction.

Again, this is all perfectly normal and natural. It's tragic that we feel we can no longer talk directly to the individual we're having those difficulties with, which is by far the best option for putting things right as soon as possible.

But that tragedy is compounded tenfold when the third party then innocently or deliberately blurts it out. This can cause emotional injury or even bitter resentment.

And it gets downright horrific when they then mistakenly or maliciously add their own damaging spin.

Human relationships of all kinds can be so tricky, don't you think? But worth such inconveniences? If they're actually worth having in the first place, absolutely!

December 12, 6.30pm – Phil has just dropped me back at my flat, having driven me over from Ferndown after an excellent day spent with the family.

He, Emily, Chloe and Harvey came to mine and we adults had hot drinks and a catch up while the youngsters messed about and watched children's TV.

Suzette also turned up with a Christmas card and present for me and stopped to have a cup of coffee. She then left to continue her day's activities and the rest of us got in Phil's car so he could take us to the Tap and Railway at West Moors for a meal.

We then went on to the Ferndown house that Em's dad Keith owned until recently signing it over to Phil.

My son and his wife now live there, along with Keith, Em's mum Gail, Em's brother Simon, Chloe, Harvey, Hamish the dog, Prince the cat and a pair of turtles called Timmy and Shelly.

All were present as I spent a few very pleasant hours there until Phil brought me back home again a short while ago.

December 16 – History was made yesterday as Major Tim Peake (43) became the first British astronaut to visit the International Space Station and the seventh UK citizen in space.

I watched the launch of the rocket he used to travel there live on TV just after 11am our time. He arrived at the ISS a few hours later to start a six-month stay as it orbits the Earth.

So I guess it's a question of ground control to Major Tim!

For myself, I had another lovely Tuesday with Paula. She came over lunch time; we had a few lagers in the Bell and then bought fish and chips on the way back to mine, where we spent the evening chilling in front of the telly.

She stayed the night and left for work early this morning. I love being with my woman, especially in her arms in bed. It makes my life complete.

I'm referring here to the companionship and partially-clothed cuddling as much as any delicious naked activities.

December 20 – Yesterday I had a very pleasant afternoon in Boscombe Conservative Club supping a few pints with my friend Lea, who I used to work for and with when I was a volunteer at Southbourne's British Red Cross charity shop.

I've explained previously how Lea and I meet up just before Christmas every year for a festive drink and catch-up.

I told her about Paula and she was delighted for me, saying I looked happier and more content than I had done in years past. She added that she badly needed my good news after the horrendous year she'd had.

Her son, Damien, now in his mid-thirties, is now disabled for life after falling 20 feet on to hard ground as he leant against a weakened wooden balcony outside his Boscombe flat's window.

He incurred arm and spinal injuries but by far the worst result was a cracked skull causing long-term brain damage that had made him confused and prone to violence.

He's kicked and punched Lea more than once since the accident in April and she's had to reluctantly ban him from staying the night at hers for her own safety.

Lea told me Damien likes his alcohol a bit too much, which only intensifies his aggressive tendencies. And he's been spending most of his money on it in the past half year or so, having lost all sense of priorities and bill paying.

He's currently living unsupervised in bed and breakfast accommodation in central Bournemouth awaiting transfer to a hostel where he can be properly looked after.

Meanwhile, Lea is on a far from merry go round involving social services, the police and solicitors drafted in to pursue a compensation claim against Damien's former landlord. Future years look like being as bleak as this one for my friend and her son.

I really feel for poor Lea, who's at the end of her tether, and Damien, who must be terrified knowing he's lost control after what's happened to him. I wish them both all the best for 2016 and beyond.

On the national stage, yesterday was the day we heard of the passing of football legend Jimmy Hill at the age of 87. He was awarded the OBE in 1984 and a CBE in 1995 for his services to the sport, on which he had a huge influence in many ways.

His diverse roles included player, coach, manager, trade union leader, director, chairman, TV executive, presenter, analyst and assistant referee. To many fans he was the face of English football with his distinctive prominent chin and goatee beard.

He started his career as a player with Brentford in 1949 but three years later moved on to Fulham, playing for them 297 times and scoring 52 goals.

As president of the Professional Footballers' Association, he successfully campaigned for an end to The Football League's maximum wage in 1961.

On hanging up his boots, he became manager of Coventry City, modernising its image while guiding it from the Third to the First Division. In 1967, he began a career in football broadcasting including many years as host of the BBC's *Match of the Day*.

RIP Jimmy – you will be missed.

December 21 – It's a cold, windy, rainy, miserable December Monday but I'm cheered by the thought that from tomorrow onwards daylight hours start to increase again. Happy Winter Solstice everyone!

December 24 – Wishing a very happy birthday to my very good pal Carole Jones, a lovely Liverpudlian I've known a long time but haven't seen face to face for many years. We are Facebook friends though, so I sent her a private message earlier today.

It's also rock legend Lemmy's 70th so happy birthday to him too.

And another footballing legend has gone to that great pitch in the sky – former England international and coach Don Howe. He died yesterday aged 80.

A full-back, he played for West Brom and Arsenal, earning 23 England caps, before establishing himself as a renowned coach for club and country.

Howe helped Arsenal to a league and FA Cup double in 1971 and spent four years as West Brom boss before returning to the Gunners as coach and manager.

He also coached under former England managers Ron Greenwood, Sir Bobby Robson and Terry Venables.

December 28 – Happy birthday to my mate Scott Collins, my great pal Kerry Smith's feller.

Well, it's the Monday after Christmas and I've had a wonderful festive weekend.

Paula came over tea-time Thursday (Christmas Eve) and after chilling for a while we headed for the Bell for a few pints of lager.

Christmas morning she drove us to her flat and we had a very pleasant three hours in the Cricketers, the lovely, friendly, homely pub close by. Then it was back to her place, where she cooked me a delicious roast dinner and we crashed out in front of the telly before having an early night as we were both tired.

Boxing Day Paula drove us back to mine and then we went off to Sam and Carl's for a few drinks with them, Diane, Tina, Jem, Rich, Bec and her boyfriend Cameron.

Yesterday (Sunday) we went to Phil and Emily's for a buffet and a few bevvies with them, my three grandchildren, Em's parents Gail and Keith and her brother Simon.

Phil, bless him, came over and picked us up then dropped us back at mine later so Paula could have a few drinks. (He had chosen not to drink himself.)

Before going to Phil's, I went on my computer to check Facebook and sent a happy birthday message to Martine, Jem's daughter.

My own Dad would have been 100 yesterday had he not died in 1984 aged 68. I still miss him terribly, kind, wise, funny man that he was.

But getting back to my weekend, it was super to spend it with people I think the world of, and especially Paula – my amazing, lovely, sexy funny Paula, who's made my Christmas and my life complete.

December 29 – Terrible news on the music front. Cancer has taken the life of rock legend Lemmy – five days after his 70th birthday. It was only diagnosed Boxing Day.

Real name Ian Kilmister, he was born in Stoke on Trent on Christmas Eve 1945.

The one-time roadie for Jimi Hendrix played in several bands before joining Hawkwind and singing the classic song Silver Machine, which reached number three in the charts in 1972.

That band fired him three years later after he was arrested in Windsor, Ontario, at the USA/Canada border on drug possession charges and spent five days in jail.

So he went on to form his own group, Motorhead, one of the finest heavy metal bands of all time that punks also loved after they toured with the Damned.

The group went from a trio to a foursome and back again through several line-up changes but Lemmy was the founder, front man and constant feature.

He carried on making records and gigging tirelessly from the seventies to this year, when Motorhead released the brilliant album Bad Magic, which I'm playing as I type.

Oh, and I have my Motorhead tee-shirt on too; I've lit a candle and put a tribute on Facebook to the great man.

Lemmy was notorious for his rock and roll lifestyle – the women, the drink and the drugs. To say he was an icon loved by millions would be a huge understatement.

Ozzy Osbourne, Brain May and Gene Simmons are among his heavy rock contemporaries delivering public eulogies since we learned of his demise yesterday.

And as reader of my previous books will know, I have my own very personal reason for being stunned and gutted. His terrific music aside, that man literally changed my life. And that is no exaggeration. RIP Lemmy – and thanks for everything.

December 31 – Wishing very happy birthdays to my friends Debi Browning, Louise Davis and Kelly Adams – and a happy new year to them and everyone else.

Paula and I are off to Sam's later to celebrate this pivotal annual turning point.

And so ends another year in the life of Martin Money and the world around him. It certainly doesn't seem 12 months ago we were last doing this.

What will the New Year bring? Who knows? But that's the glorious unpredictability of existence in this crazy reality.

Some may consider my slant on things decidedly bizarre and quite frankly mad.

But are my theories and opinions any stranger than other people's – especially those of the millions convinced that a virgin gave birth to a baby that grew into a man who was then executed but rose from the dead three days later?

Given that scenario, widely accepted without question the world over, are the notions of alien visitors, a self-obsessed, cruel, sinister shadow government ruling us or our actually being at the mercy of cold-blooded reptiles really all that more implausible?

I'd suggest that to answer yes would display a remarkable level of intellectual confusion and amazing ability to hold two contradictory views at the same time.

I've long given up on boldly declaring any belief in rigid and inflexible paradigms. I leave that to tunnel-visioned and arrogant fools.

I keep an open mind while posing possible explanations, that's all. Some may agree with me. Many will not. That's the way the cookie crumbles I suppose.

I must stress here that I'm certainly not knocking anyone's religious views. Neither do I intend disrespect causing any offence.

I'm just saying there are different ways of looking at things. Each to their own, live and let live and all that.

So it just remains for me to bring this book to a close by wishing everyone happiness, health and prosperity in 2016. Methinks it's time for the last chapter…

****

CHAPTER ELEVEN – TO WRAP IT UP

The past year has been dreadful for many people – death and destruction across the globe, tragic events in my life and those of family and friends and generally speaking a whole load of pain and hassle for millions, probably billions.

But I've had some great times with loved ones and mates all the same. Thanks everyone from the bottom of my heart.

And, brilliantly out of the blue, I've become reunited with a woman I've loved for 20 years – when I'd long given up on ever being in a relationship or this happy again.

It's said that we all yearn for a happy ending. Paula's providing me with mine. This one's especially for you babe.

Ta ta folks

Peace and love

The entity labelled Martin Money, December 31, 2015

****

"One does not ask of one who suffers: What is your country and what is your religion? One merely says: You suffer, that is enough for me" – Louis Pasteur.

"We will travel home in a new reality, not a new Ferrari" – David Icke.

Illusions only have power over you if you believe them to be real.

Sometimes we all need to say sorry for the things we've said and done. But no-one should ever apologize for being who they are, the views they hold or the way they lead their life – as long as they don't cause too much pain and hurt to others along the way.

We should all try constantly to be better people, but those who can't accept and respect us for us – inconsistencies, insecurities, irrational fears, irritating traits, warts, flaws and all – should keep the hell away.

I'm a sort of cross between Bridget Jones, Samuel Pepys and Tim Rice.

Technology and me just don't mix – I still struggle with the concept of pencils!

In any sphere of life, when the bad times outweigh the good, you should make your exit and find pastures new.

This book is written in loving memory of my Auntie Joyce, who passed over just after I started writing it.

For my mate Andy claimed by cancer a few days after his 51st birthday: Celtic Nicky.

And rock legend Lemmy, a man who changed my life more than most.

Plus Mum, Dad, Uncles Fred, Jack and Bert, Aunties Joan and Sylvia, my son John and other relatives and friends already on the next level.

It is dedicated to my cousins Sandra, Eric, Colin, John and Andrew plus their partners, spouses and children.

To Carol, David, Lisa, Kevin, Jamie, Richard, Ruth, Liam, Dylan, Scott, Jane, Isabelle, Joshua, Lottie and Jonathan. Plus our "adopted sister" Suzette.

And of course – as always – to Phil, Emily, Chloe, Lucas and Harvey.

To my soul mate, best pal and lover Paula, happily back in my life after far too long. Love you to the stars and back, babe.

And to my wider family, to Joe, Dawn and my brilliant friends of both sexes. Big thanks for the affection, kindness, laughs and wonderful memories.

Wishing each and every one of you love, peace, and happiness

M.M.

ABOUT THE AUTHOR

Born in Slough on February 25, 1954, Martin Money lived there until early adulthood, moving to Dorset in 1978.

Leaving school with three A Levels and seven O Levels, he worked in a bank for a few months before starting a 24-year career in regional journalism that ended in redundancy in 1997.

Since then he's had a variety of part-time jobs and also worked as a volunteer for charities.

A proud father and grandfather, he lives in Bournemouth where he enjoys short cliff-top walks, writing, reading, watching TV, listening to music and socialising.

Author's photo by Sam Excell

www.ingramcontent.com/pod-product-compliance
Lightning Source LLC
Chambersburg PA
CBHW031122250726
48655CB00004B/1808